Solomon says "a friend loves at all times and a brother was born for adversity." Whatever else is true of pastoral ministry, it is true that it will always come with its share of trials and difficulties. This book calls pastors to prepare for this reality by forming friendships—forming brotherhoods—with other pastors, so together they can bless, equip, and encourage one another. I believe every pastor will benefit from reading it and following its counsel.

Tim Challies
Author, *Seasons of Sorrow*

I have long been concerned about the epidemic of sectarianism and pastoral isolation in the church of Jesus Christ. Addressing this epidemic, Joel Littlefield encourages gospel-centered ministers to pursue kingdom-mindedness by cultivating friendship and fellowship with one another, then offers practical guidance for creating healthy, Christ-centered, and edifying pastoral coalitions. May the irenic spirit of which Littlefield speaks prevail in our day for the sake of Christ and His kingdom!

Joel Beeke
Chancellor and Professor, Puritan Reformed Theological Seminary, Grand Rapids, Michigan

The kingdom of Christ is bigger than your church, pastor. Part of being kingdom-minded, therefore, is learning how to partner with and encourage other pastors in your area. Joel Littlefield's enthusiasm for pastors partnering together just may point you to a crucial aspect of kingdom ministry you've missed. Then he offers practical counsel for pursuing such partnerships – for the good of your own pastorate and church as well as for the advance of the kingdom.

Jonathan Leeman
Editorial Director, 9Marks

Kingdom-minded pastors recognize there is no place in the ministry for a Lone Ranger. We all need a band of brothers who come alongside to encourage, admonish, instruct and challenge us in the high calling of Christian ministry. This book will show you both the importance and the how of forming a group of likeminded men for the fight we engage as ministers of Christ. Take it to heart and put it into action.

Danny Akin
President, Southeastern Baptist Theological Seminary,
Wake Forest, North Carolina

Joel Littlefield has given us a helpful, practical, and interesting book to map out ways that pastors can offer and receive encouragement from fellow pastors. *The Kingdom-Minded Pastor* cuts to the chase and gives workable strategies for building a coalition of pastors in a local community who will join arms to multiply gospel work. I encourage you to read this book and to put its message into practice.

Phil Newton
Director of Pastoral Care and Mentoring, The Pillar Network
Wake Forest, North Carolina;

The friendship of other brothers in pastoral ministry is one of the reasons why many pastors are still in pastoral ministry today. More than that, such friendships stimulate, encourage, inform and enrich a pastor's ministry in ways that bears fruit way beyond the regular realm of one's own ministry. This is why Joel's book is a gift to those who operate as lone rangers. Make time to read it, and make time to do it ... for the Kingdom.

Liam Garvie
Associate Pastor, Charlotte Chapel,
Edinburgh

Amidst the stormy seas of tribalism within the evangelical church, Joel Littlefield offers us a life raft in the form of gospel-centred pastoral coalitions. While many of us may find ourselves ministering alone and with little kingdom-making impact, Littlefield presents a worked-out plea for pastors to form a band of brothers which will enable us to go deeper for the sake the kingdom. When the church is facing an epidemic of discouragement, Joel calls us to the readily available vaccine of kingdom-minded togetherness. This short book packs a punch and can be quickly read by an individual or be poured over and debated by a group. I have a sense that this may spark off a renewed movement of doctrinally-aligned and missionally-driven pastors.

David C. Meredith
Mission Director, Free Church of Scotland

The Kingdom-Minded Pastor is a groundbreaking, yet ageless guide for pastors, urging them to unite with like-minded peers to foster vibrant, flourishing communities of faith springing forth from their own dedication to kingdom living. By championing fellowship and intentional relationships, this book equips pastors to lead with resilience, prioritize self-care, embrace courage and fulfill the Great Commission. Littlefield's work is must-read for pastors committed to seeing God's kingdom come on earth through the embodied beauty of Christian community.

Robert Smith, Jr.
Charles T. Carter Baptist Chair of Divinity, Beeson Divinity School, Samford University, Birmingham, Alabama

THE
KINGDOM
MINDED
PASTOR

**How Pastoral Partnership
Advances the Kingdom**

Joel Littlefield

Foreword by Brian Croft

CHRISTIAN
FOCUS

Practical
Shepherding

paperback ISBN 978-1-5271-1170-7
ebook ISBN 978-1-5271-1179-0

Published in 2024
by
Christian Focus Publications Ltd,
Geanies House, Fearn, Ross-shire,
IV20 1TW, Scotland
www.christianfocus.com
with
Practical Shepherding, Inc,
P.O. Box 21806, Louisville, Kentucky 40221, USA
www.practicalshepherding.com

Cover design by Daniel van Straaten

Printed and bound by Bell & Bain, Glasgow.

Contents

FOREWORD

Discouragement seems to be an epidemic among pastors today. This stems from many factors, one of the most common of which is loneliness. Pastors are notorious for isolating themselves in their churches and ministries. As a result, they are continually tempted to think they are the only ones who face the pressures and demands of the ministry.

The antidote to much of this discouragement can be found in deliberate and purposeful fellowship with other pastors. Not just any pastors, but likeminded pastors. Fostering this kind of fellowship was our aim when I started a pastoral fellowship over ten years ago with three pastor friends, which we now call *The Pastoral Fellowship for Practical Theology*.

Very early in my ministry I was taught the importance of fellowship with other pastors. So when Jim, one of my dear pastor friends, approached me about getting a pastors' fellowship started, I was very interested. We knew this would be a good idea for several reasons, but one that leaped to our minds was the fact that Jim and I each had our own network of pastors we knew but the other did not. So, Jim and I agreed to each include one more pastor we knew well and trusted, and who we thought might be interested in meeting together to discuss the possibilities.

With the other two men we agreed to include, we began to meet once a month to get to know each other, fellowship together, pray for one another, and discuss whether a pastors' fellowship was a wise and likely fruitful venture. We agreed it would be a beneficial opportunity to meet and encourage other pastors. But we also realized the four of us each strategically pastored in the four corners of the city of Louisville, Kentucky, and each of us knew likeminded pastors the others did not. Thus began the leadership team that would launch *The Pastoral Fellowship for Practical Theology.*

As we began to discuss who to invite, we realized we had to form a template that would allow us to rally pastors who are likeminded in what we consider essential areas of agreement, without being too rigid and thereby alienating pastors in need unnecessarily. We came to agree on these four main tenants to determine those who would be invited:

1. A commitment to the biblical gospel of Jesus Christ.
2. A commitment to expositional preaching as the steady diet of a congregation.
3. A commitment to the centrality of the local church.

4. A commitment to the call of the pastor to shepherd the souls of his people as one who will give an account.

Although members of our group hold various positions regarding polity, baptism, and reformed theology, we decided that disagreements over these issues could coexist with enough like-mindedness to make the fellowship meaningful. We also limited the invitation list to full-time and bi-vocational pastors, lay elders, and associate pastors; we suspected that the inclusion of pastoral interns and pastors-in-training might limit transparency. This is a parameter we still follow. We continue to meet five times a year, and have been for over a decade now. And we continue to have over 200 pastors involved in this fellowship, with approximately 45-50 who attend each meeting.

Unexpected Fruit

These times together have borne some unexpected fruits: I will mention two.

First, although the four pastors who started this fellowship hoped for increased affections for the others through this time, we would all confess how surprisingly deep our love for the others has grown. On the off months when our fellowship does not meet, the four of us have breakfast together to minister to each other. Without exception, the Lord meets us by his Spirit in very sweet and unexpected ways each time the four of us meet.

The second surprise is how far some pastors travel for our meetings and how many have connected with other pastors they had no idea were near them. As a result, they have begun meeting regularly on their own. The way this time has multiplied other spin-off groups has been a huge encouragement to us and an unexpected joy.

It is this kind of encouragement and unexpected joy that I desire for every pastor, which is why I am so thankful for this book you hold in your hands. Joel Littlefield is doing this same kind of kingdom-minded work. I've seen it. I've been a part of it. But he is doing it in a uniquely hard, dark, place on the soil of New England. This demonstrates that if God can work through the partnership and fellowship of pastors in a dark place like Maine, then God can work in your area too. What I appreciate about this book is that Joel shares his insights not just on why pastors should partner and fellowship with other pastors, but, specifically, how to do it.

Through *The Pastoral Fellowship for Practical Theology* in Louisville, Kentucky, all of us involved with it have been reminded of something very important: pastors are discouraged, and they need each other. We may pastor individual churches, but we are all called to the same under-shepherding task, and we will answer to the same Chief Shepherd (1 Pet. 5:4). The more we can lock arms and spur one another on to be steadfast until the Chief Shepherd appears, the better off every pastor will be on that day.

That includes you, pastor. So read this book with a pen and highlighter. Take notes. Read it with a few pastor friends in your local area. Put these wise, practical suggestions into practice. Then watch and be amazed at how God might work through you and other pastors who desire the same thing—Christ's return and God's kingdom come.

Brian Croft
Executive Director
Practical Shepherding
January 2024

INTRODUCTION

If you are like me, then you desire to see a movement of God in your community. You want men, women, and children to surrender to the Lordship of Christ through the regenerating work of the Spirit. You want new churches planted, declining churches revitalized, and for your own congregation to be about the work of making disciples of Christ. It is going to require nothing less than the power of God to do this. Apart from Him we can do nothing. Many churches today are spinning their wheels, burning out, and getting nowhere for the kingdom. Some of this weakness can be attributed to pastors who are disconnected from fellowship with other pastors.

This book is about an aspect of pastoral ministry that many do not think about. I'm going to try to convince you that being kingdom-minded is an imperative for your soul, your family, the church you serve, and the community you desire to reach with the gospel. Much of the information in this book is highly practical in nature. It will impact the everyday mission and vision of the local church. We need that.

I believe that a pastor with a kingdom mindset is a force to be reckoned with. He understands that he is better off in partnership with other pastors. He understands that multiplication is at the heart of Great Commission work. He understands that collaboration with other like-minded leaders is not a sign of incompetence, but of Christlike humility, and obedience. There is a collective potential that exists in every community on this earth where the gospel is being preached, because in every community, there are spiritual shepherds who are in need of strength, encouragement, training, and missional realignment.

Week in and week out, pastors are teaching and discipling people to be in regular fellowship. We teach it because we believe it. Continuing steadfastly in prayer, communion, teaching, and fellowship are all part of being a fruitful Christian that gives glory to God. Although it is true that pastors and elders can find strength in the fellowship of their own church family (and they should), there is a unique benefit found in the company of other pastors. The kind of fellowship and cooperation among pastors that I am arguing for in this book is rooted in intentional kingdom decisions and gospel-saturated mission. The goal is to align with the mission and mindset of our Lord. He desires to multiply the kingdom on earth through the church, and the leaders He calls.

If we are to see awakening and revival, I believe that pastors need to lead the way. May you find this book to be both practical and motivating. It's quite simple. I want you to be active in the starting, joining, and nurturing of intentional pastors' coalitions. A coalition is an alliance for joint action. There are pastors in your city or town that you can partner with. Intentional kingdom-minded relationships will, Lord willing, result in healthier pastors, healthier local churches, and kingdom multiplication.*

---

* This is likely a challenge most particularly felt for pastors within baptistic denominations; nonetheless, the goal for these pastoral coalitions are cross-denominational.

It's important for pastors to get together. That's my big takeaway from my time in our pastor's coalition. To be with others that know the burdens of ministry, the ups and the downs, and are currently facing the same things that you are week in and week out is invaluable. We apply Hebrew 10:24-25 to the gathering of the body, but I often leave our coalition gatherings thinking about it's application to the gathering of pastors. There's something that happens when pastors gather. We are "stirred up" as the text says. We sort of awaken from the stupor that comes with week in/week out ministry and are given fresh motivation to pursue the "love and good works" that make our ministries thrive. But we don't get that if we neglect the gathering. That's why I'm grateful for this group: it stirs my heart and my mind, and I leave encouraged and motivated to shepherd the flock the Lord has entrusted to me with greater faithfulness.

Aaron Manning
Fort Hill Community Church, Gorham, Maine
Member of the Isaac Case Coalition

1

SOMETHING NEEDS TO CHANGE

The kingdom-minded pastor understands that no church or pastor can do the work of the Great commission alone. A kingdom-minded pastor is not as concerned with territorial control as he is with saturating all places with the gospel. The kingdom-minded pastor values partnership with others. I believe that, by discussing partnerships between pastors, we are diving into a subject that is close to Christ's heart. Are you ready to make the shift, to embrace a new paradigm in ministry? Let us face the necessary changes to become healthier local pastors, leading healthier local churches. First, we need to admit that there are problems.

Problem #1: The Lonely Pastor

> There he came to a cave and lodged in it. And behold, the word of the LORD came to him, and he said to him, "What are you doing here, Elijah?" He said, "I have been very jealous for the LORD, the God of hosts. For the people of Israel have forsaken your covenant, thrown down your altars, and killed your prophets with the sword, and I, even I only, am left, and they seek my life, to take it away. (1 Kings 19:9-10)

If we're going to become more kingdom-minded in our pastoral ministry, we will need to acknowledge that there are things that need to change. Change is hard. Knowing that there are problems and never addressing them is destructive. In this chapter, I want to help you identify a few key problems that tend to get in the way. Let's start with isolation and loneliness. Everyone faces times of loneliness. It could come from neglect, abandonment, or the feelings that come from being ridiculed by others. This can push a person into isolation. Loneliness can also be self-afflicted. Some personalities have a harder time forming healthy relationships. Introverted people need to work hard to come out of their shell, to be exposed to the life-giving effects of fellowship and friendship. All of this is true for every human on earth, including pastors.

Pastoral ministry is a heavy burden to bear. Shepherds have the job of leading, loving, nurturing, and disciplining a flock of sheep for the sake of their spiritual good and safety. This can be lonely work for a variety of reasons. Church members treat their leaders as though they have no needs, even if such treatement is unintentional. It's true that pastors should be competent in self-leadership, but this does not mean that pastors have no weaknesses or needs of their own.

A pastor can experience loneliness in his own denomination or network of churches. Looking back, the family of churches that I was involved with as a new Christian has provided me with a good comparison. Before I was ever a pastor, I witnessed church planters go out from the mother church. Over time, the pastors and families who started those new churches began to experience loneliness. They were in an unfamiliar place. They lacked the committed community they once enjoyed. They were on their way to building a new church family, but it would take time. The need for connection, friendship, encouragement, and partnership does not gone away.

Consider Paul's words to the church that he planted in Philippi:

> I thank my God in all my remembrance of you, always in every prayer of mine for you all making my prayer with joy, because of your partnership in the gospel from the first day until now. And I am sure of this, that he who began a good work in you will bring it to completion at the day of Jesus Christ. (Phil. 1:4-6)

The Philippian church was prayed for, loved, and remembered by Paul. They were not neglected or left to fend for themselves, as I fear many pastors and new church plants are today.

Problem #2: Stagnant Mission and Ministry

> I know your works: you are neither cold nor hot. Would that you were either cold or hot! (Rev. 3:15)

Another problem I often see is when a local church has grown stagnant in their mission. These are usually churches with a leader who knows that important changes are necessary, but the leadership muscle is too weak to make those changes. This is often the case in a church with a single pastor. He has been called to revitalize the church. The deacon board is calling the shots, but their decisions are not motivated by a biblical mission. They have little respect for the pastoral office because tradition has convinced them that they are in charge. They believe the pastor must bend to their wishes. This scenario is common, and churches are dying as a result. It could also be that the existing members have been scared by the actions of previous pastors, so they offer the new hire little trust. This is a stagnant church. It cannot move forward with a kingdom vision because the leadership structure is unhealthy. You might be that lone pastor who feels like you are fighting against your deacons and members, rather than working together in harmony. Many are walking in similar shoes. This can change, but you will need patience and boldness. Hold on.

Sometimes the church is stuck because the pastor is stuck in his pride and refusing to heed the signs of decline. He needs to lead the church in a direction that fits a thoroughly biblical model, but he won't. There's no intentional discipleship, no fellowship happening beyond Sunday morning, the sermons are always topical (they should never be always topical) and rarely expositional, the youth are gone, and leaders are not being developed for future eldership. This is what I see as I look around my region.

I live in a small community in Maine with a population of around nine thousand people. Even in this small community I see stagnancy. Maine was once a land of rich gospel fruitfulness. I'll be dedicating the final chapter of this book to introducing you to two inspiring figures in church history, one of which made an impact on my own state. Many of the churches that pepper this land are no longer filled with healthy Christians or being led by qualified pastors. The Great Commission of Christ is omitted. The numbers are clear. Churches are declining and church doors are closing. We need to shock the system back to life with a good dose of kingdom-mindedness. Look at the words of Christ to a small local church in ancient day Asia Minor, perhaps a lot like yours: "I know your works. You have the reputation of being alive, but you are dead. Wake up, and strengthen what remains and is about to die, for I have not found your works complete in the sight of my God" (Rev. 3:1-2). The reputation of being alive is not good enough. Wake up, my brothers!

Problem #3: Heavy Burdens

> I am not able to carry all this people alone; the burden is too heavy for me ... Then the LORD said to Moses, "Gather for me seventy men of the elders of Israel, whom you know to be the elders of the people and officers over them, and bring them to the tent of meeting, and let them take their stand there with you" (Num. 11:14, 16).

Moses's burden was too heavy to carry alone. Kingdom-minded pastors bear a weight that seminary training can hardly prepare them for. We will all find ourselves in situations like Moses from time to time when we are at the end of our own strength and need others to stand with us. We all need the wisdom found in faithful friends and counselors who are walking in similar shoes and bearing similar burdens.

Look around you. I'm sure you know a pastor who is carrying a heavy load. His marriage is struggling because the ministry is taking up all his time, and he struggles to say no. He and his wife have not been on a date without kids for five years. You know of the pastor I'm speaking about. He hears complaints from members who don't like his preaching. He doesn't have an elder team to support and encourage him. He's the brother whose family decided to step into the difficult world of adoption, and now they are church planting with no support system. The church is falling apart due to disunity and infighting. Paul, likewise, carried a heavy-burden, as described in his second letter to the Corinthian church:

> Five times I received at the hands of the Jews the forty lashes less one. Three times I was beaten with rods. Once I was stoned. Three times I was shipwrecked; a night and a day I was adrift at sea; on frequent journeys, in danger from rivers, danger from robbers, danger from my own people, danger from Gentiles, danger in the city, danger in the wilderness, danger at sea, danger from false brothers; in toil and hardship, through many a sleepless night, in hunger and thirst, often without food, in cold and exposure. And, apart from other things, there is the daily pressure on me of my anxiety for all the churches. Who is weak, and I am not weak? Who is made to fall, and I am not indignant? (2 Cor. 11:24-29)

Paul carried a heavy burden. He thought about the churches he had planted over the years. He loved them. He cared about their leaders and the congregations. He wanted them to grow in Christ and to multiply. Paul's list teaches us that we are not alone in the burdens we bear. Paul's burdens outnumber mine ten to one, and I hear no complaining from him. But we also learn from this that Paul had a vested interest in the life of more than just one church. He cared for them all. That's kingdom-mindedness. With the inevitability of burdens, you need as many as you can get standing by your side. You need your wife, children, church members, and fellow elders. You need the unique and fresh perspective that pastors of other local churches can bring you. There are people around you (even if you haven't found them yet) with wisdom to share.

Again, the life and ministry of Moses gives us a good example. In Exodus 18, Moses had already led the Israelites out of Egypt as God freed them from slavery. After crossing the Red Sea and wandering in the wilderness, the people are in need of council. Day and night, they come to Moses to receive his wisdom. Yet his father-in-law, Jethro, recognizes that this is too much a burden for one man to carry himself. Receiving Jethro's instruction, Moses gathers leaders together from each tribe, placing them in leadership over thousands, hundreds, fifties, and tens, that the burden might be shouldered together. The burden of leadership is one which ought to be shared and carried together, arm in arm, with fellow brothers in Christ, lest we overburden ourselves.

Problem #4: Lacking Intentionality

And let us consider how to stir up one another to love and good works, not neglecting to meet together, as is the habit of some, but encouraging one another, and all the more as you see the Day drawing near (Heb. 10:24-25).

This New Testament text is commonly used to encourage fellowship and attendance for believers in the local church, but the principle applies to pastor-to-pastor relationships as well. One of the purposes of this book is to convince you that meeting with an intentional group of likeminded pastors can positively affect your life and ministry. One might reply, "Yes, but I've been to pastors' meetings before, and it was a waste of my time." We don't need more meetings so that pastors can come together and complain. I attended a few in 2020 during that dreaded COVID year. Pastors needed encouragement at that time more than ever. To my disappointment, the conversations never seemed to get past, "How many people are wearing masks in your church?" or "How is your online attendance?" Those questions are not innately wrong. When addressed with a kingdom mindset, they can be used for equipping and encouragement. Nevertheless, we need our meetings to be intentional for the kingdom and for the encouragement of a pastor's soul. We need meetings that allow pastors to engage in matters of deep soul-searching, biblical discussion, and meaningful prayer. We need to be able to share the unique struggles we face as shepherds, pointing each other to the hope and faithfulness of our great Shepherd.

It's Not All Bad News

Before we move on, let's rejoice in the fact that there are pastors and churches who are doing well. I hope that you are one of those. I hope that, as you read this, you are not on the brink of burnout. I hope that you can say that the Lord is good to you, and that ministry, though always challenging, is a blessing in your life because Jesus is good. Even though pastoral ministry is guaranteed to be trying, I pray that you are experiencing the fullness of God's joy. I believe that right now in most communities there are men who are committed to the Scriptures. There are men who will teach and apply a biblical vision even when it costs them greatly. There are men who are committed to shepherding their flocks. There are men who are standing on biblical truth and committed to developing leaders, planting new churches, and fulfilling the Great Commission. These are the kind of men you need fellowship with. If you do find yourself in a good and healthy place right now, let me challenge you to step up and encourage another pastor today.

To the lonely pastor reading this book, the Lord loves you. You are never truly alone. Remember to preach this to yourself daily. Do not allow your weary soul to suffer in silence any longer. Cling to Jesus and the help He has graciously supplied for you in the truth of the gospel. Remember that His Spirit indwells you. His Word is sufficient for you. You are His adopted son, and He calls you friend. Don't wallow in self-pity. Ask the Spirit of God to search your heart. There may be sin there that you need to repent from. Sins of self-sufficiency, distrust, unforgiveness, and bitterness can easily cloud one's ability to see the will of God. It may be the need to forgive those who have neglected, slandered, or abandoned you, leading you to isolate yourself. Begin to build your confidence again in God's vision for the church.

Whatever your unique circumstance, I rejoice over you. I want you to be the pioneers for kingdom-minded partnership in your church, city, or region. Fixing the problems identified in this chapter begins with having the right vision. Stagnant churches and lonely pastors, whose arms are weak from carrying the burden alone, will continue to be a problem until a vision for kingdom-mindedness takes center stage.

Questions for Further Consideration:

1. Several problems were mentioned in this chapter. Which one can you most identify with?

2. What could you do to encourage a pastor who is discouraged and tired, and help to strengthen him?

3. As you consider your current mission field, what factors do you believe are hindering the fruitfulness of local churches, including your own?

It's really helpful for me to know that I'm connected to a greater work of the Lord outside of our local church. I never want to be a pastor on an island by myself and this group is great in helping me see other men carrying and proclaiming the same gospel. So, the primary benefit for me is on a pastoral level. Plus the fellowship is really refreshing to my soul, which does spill into all other areas of my life. I honestly can't think of any way this could be better.

John Andrade
Church Planting in Portland, Maine
Member of the Isaac Case Coalition

2

A Kingdom Vision

Part 1 – What does it look like?

A kingdom vision begins with believing and knowing that Christ is the King. The kingdom of Heaven has come to this earth in the person and work of Jesus. He announced its arrival. It has already happened. Believing this is essential for pastors because if Christ is not ruling and reigning today, then by whose authority do we preach? There is another reality that we must accept. We are still waiting for the consummation of His Kingship. That is when death is put away forever, and all believers finally come together in a new Heaven and a new Earth. Theologians call this the "now and not yet" reality of the kingdom. I think far too many Christians, and pastors, spend too much time thinking about the not yet—but the "now" is crucial. Having a kingdom vision means that we are confident in the authority and Kingship of Jesus in this world, over the universe, and over our ministries. It's being confident in the success of our mission because of our confidence in our King, Jesus.

Small Is Formidable in the Kingdom

The kingdom of God and the work that promotes the growth of His kingdom start small. Jesus compared them to a mustard seed, saying,

> The kingdom of heaven is like a grain of mustard seed that a man took and sowed in his field. It is the smallest of all seeds, but when it has grown it is larger than all the garden plants and becomes a tree, so that the birds of the air come and make nests in its branches (Matt. 13:31-32).

There's nothing impressive about mustard seeds. It is only when the seed is planted that it will begin to work towards its fullest potential. Over time it grows. Over time the roots will go down deeper. Eventually, the mustard seed grows to overshadow the whole garden. How it began was not how it was intended to stay. There is much we can learn from this parable about our work in the kingdom. We know that small is formidable in the kingdom of God. The Devil would like us all to believe that small means weak, insignificant, and unimportant. We know better.

Small Can Be Discouraging

The often small and seemingly insignificant nature of kingdom work can be discouraging. It has discouraged me at times in my ministry. Near the end of time, when the gospel has covered the whole earth and all the nations have been discipled, this parable will be fully understood. But God allows us to see smaller fulfillments of these kingdom principles to remind us that Jesus's words are true. Our perseverance is not wasted.

Several years ago, when my wife and I planted the church that we currently serve in, I had to remind myself that even though the crowd was small, the funds were small, and that not everyone shared the same enthusiasm that we did, Jesus was still working. God wanted us to be faithful in the small things first before receiving greater responsibilities. Misunderstanding this kingdom principle has been the discouragement and downfall of many. Small teams, small attendance, small towns, few leaders, and few responses to the preaching of the gospel is a reality everywhere. But if we believe the principle of the parable of the mustard seed, then we know that the season of small does not mean insignificant and weak.

Be Faithful in the Small Things

Be faithful in the small things and you will be entrusted with greater things. Faithfulness to God in this current season of your ministry might look different than what you originally thought. Listen to how Paul called Timothy to faithfulness to the kingdom. "I charge you in the presence of God and of Christ Jesus, who is to judge the living and the dead, and by his appearing and his kingdom: preach the word; be ready in season and out of season; reprove, rebuke, and exhort, with complete patience and teaching" (2 Tim. 4:1-2). Can you hear the kingdom principles in this exhortation? Keep preaching. Be faithful to the Scriptures whether your congregation is small or large, whether people oppose you or rejoice over you, whether you have a team of leaders to support you or not. Wait patiently for growth. Labor in prayer. Do all this with a focus on the King and His kingdom.

Did you see Paul's words about the kingdom in the text? "I charge you in the presence of God...by His *appearing* and His *kingdom*." This is the now and the not yet. Jesus has already appeared. He revealed himself in all His glory to three of His disciples. He healed the sick, cast out demons, and displayed to the world that all authority in Heaven and Earth are truly His. He proved all His kingdom claims by dying and rising from the grave. Considering these things, be faithful in your season. There is a day coming when He will appear again. He will consummate the kingdom and crush all remaining effects of sin and evil. Considering these things, be faithful in your season. Just like Timothy, your perseverance comes from believing that the rule of Christ's kingdom is a reality right now, and a future promise to cling to. Remember the principle of the mustard seed parable. Small is formidable because when Christians walk in the strength which Christ supplies, we walk in His kingdom authority. Small is formidable because God's strength is made perfect in our weaknesses. Do not despise the day of small things. Embrace the season. Enjoy the season. This is all part of developing a kingdom vision.

It's Bigger Than Just You
Keep in mind that you are not the only pastor around. This is a good thing. Pastors can suffer from tunnel vision in ministry. We tend to keep our focus on our sermons, our plans, and our dreams. If I'm honest, I possess a bit of this myself. When we planted New City Church in 2017, I had a big vision. I was going to execute it with or without the help of others. Most of the church planting books I was told to read, including the assessment I went through, told me that to be entrepreneurial was a common characteristic of successful church planters. That was me. Thankfully, I had mentor figures in my life to help me see my shortcomings. Do you have the tendency of thinking that your gifts and skills are all that God needs? The Scriptures teach us that the kingdom of God consists of many laborers. There are many who are laboring in your community right now. There are pastors who are praying, studying, dreaming, and seeking every day to be obedient to the Great Commission of Christ. A pastor with a kingdom vision will admit that the success of his ministry requires the work of other pastors and other congregations. We are only a small piece of the whole picture God is painting.

Part 2: Characteristics of Our King
We Need His Humility
One thing we notice when reading the New Testament is the humility of Christ. His ambition was not driven

by a desire for fame, but for the glory of the Father through the laying down of His life. Jesus said, "But whoever would be great among you must be your servant, and whoever would be first among you must be your slave, even as the Son of Man came not to be served but to serve, and to give his life as a ransom for many" (Matt. 20:26-28). Think about the ambition of the average person today. When someone is ambitious about success, the tendency is to forget about personal character, integrity, and the good of those around them. Pastors are not immune to this sin. The desire to lead a ministry that reaches the masses, to be a world class preacher, or to display that PhD certificate in your office can quickly become something impure. Do you desire success for yourself alone, or for the kingdom? Ambition is good. Aspirations are good. To leave these unchecked is dangerous to yourself and to others. Jesus had great ambition that did not push others aside. His ambition was not selfish or conceited. He came into this world with a clear mission to seek and save the lost. He was confident, perfect, and entrusted Himself to the Father. In all of this He did no wrong. His ambition never clouded His compassion. His Disciples never experienced the cold shoulder, a bad attitude, or a complaint. Our King had humble ambition, and the kingdom-minded pastor will desire the same.

We Need His Servant Nature

Christ was the ultimate servant. Paul puts it this way: "Have this mind among yourselves, which is yours in Christ Jesus, who, though he was in the form of God, did not count equality with God a thing to be grasped, but emptied himself, by taking the form of a servant, being born in the likeness of men. And being found in human form, he humbled himself by becoming obedient to the point of death, even death on a cross" (Phil. 2:5-8). Servanthood is a common grace from God in this world that helps us to understand what He is like. Think of how different our world would be if nobody served. Parents would neglect their children completely; nurses and doctors would not exist; there would be no military willing to serve for their countrymen, and so on. The fact that people serve selflessly in these capacities, and others, is evidence of our being created in the image of God. Despite this common and beautiful grace, the biblical understanding of servanthood is counterintuitive to most of the world. The pastor needs to be ever aware of this and seek to emulate Christ's servant nature in life and ministry.

In the passage above, Paul teaches us that Jesus *took the form of a servant* to accomplish His mission. I'll skim the surface just enough to remind you of something important when it comes to developing a kingdom vision. Jesus, the Son of God, was once without human flesh. Before His birth in Bethlehem, Jesus was not a physical being. His incarnation was the beginning of something incredible, but not the beginning of His existence. Paul tells us that, "He was in the form of God", but he chose a different form when coming to earth, the human form. Since we have only ever known human existence, we must work hard to comprehend this. Christ traveled an immeasurable distance from the realm of eternal glory and perfection to the realm of the finite and sinful. He could have come in the clouds of heaven, arrayed in splendor like a King. He could have arrived on a chariot of fire, ready to conquer His enemies. He chose to enter our world through birth, just like the rest of us. He chose to be born in a poor town, in a barn, to sinful parents, and none of it was without purpose. None of it was random. The Scriptures are clear that the reason He became one of us, was not only to live the life we could never live, but that he might die the death which we deserved. By taking on the form of a man, Jesus opened Himself up to all the effects of a sinful and broken world, including the most humiliating and gruesome death in history. Paul called this "the form of a servant". It was His servant-heartedness that ultimately led to our salvation.

Dying to Self

There's one more thing I want to draw out regarding our King to help us develop a kingdom vision. This is a truth that my heart needs to hear daily as a Christian and as a pastor. Jesus has bid me to come and die, just as He came and died. He's not asking that I go to the cross the way He did and pay for my own sins. That's not possible. But He is asking that I lay down my life. Jesus taught that anyone who desires to follow Him must first deny himself, then pick up his cross and follow. Baptism is a great picture of this. Baptism is a public profession of faith, a visible entering of a believer into the death, burial, and resurrection of Christ. Through baptism, we proclaim to the church and the world that our life is hidden with Christ in God, that we have died to sin, and we are alive to God. We now identify with a new way. Up becomes down, and down becomes up. The one who loses his life is the one that saves it, and the one who holds on to it is the one who loses it in the end. Having been saved by Christ, we are forgiven and free, but there is still sin that remains that must be crucified. The penalty of sin is gone, but the power of sin and its effects are felt. The working out of our salvation includes dying daily and clinging to the hope of the gospel. Christ died to self in the ultimate sense. Gethsemane vividly portrayed the will of the Son of God humbly relenting to the will of His Father. Before He died on Calvary, He crucified the inner human will that wanted, even if just for a moment, the easier path. Our Lord died for us so that we might live. I'm painting a picture of a need that we all have as Christians. Based on the exemplary life that leaders have been called to live, it's especially important that pastors understand this.

How Should We Respond?

Pastors need a mind that is saturated in the humility of Christ. Only when we are humble in ministry can we see that our purpose is not the glory of self, but the glory of God. The kingdom-minded pastor humbly recognizes that the work of the Great Commission today, and its ultimate future fulfillment, is due to the combined faithfulness of many, and the singular faithfulness of God.

The kingdom-minded pastor is emulating Christ by taking the form of a servant in his personal and ministerial life. Start with your family. Be diligent in this, brothers. Your wives need you to serve for their sake and for the sake of your children. Remember that the one with real authority is the one who is under the authority of Christ. I mention this first because your kingdom-efforts must never neglect the health of your family. It must begin there. With your home in order, look at your mission field and consider the people who are serving around you in your city. Begin to look past your own abilities and see your need for others.

The servant nature of our Savior is yours through the indwelling Spirit. It is also a gift that needs to be developed. One thing we learn about Christ from the Scriptures is that He is a burden-bearer. He bids us come to him with all our burdens. He bears up the heaviest of our yokes, the yoke of our sin. As we walk with him, learn from Him, and pay close attention, we will learn how to bear the burdens of others, and, in this case, become an immense blessing to other pastors.

Finally, do not miss the fact that the pastor holds a sacrificial office. There are many implications to this truth, including dying to certain comforts and dreams, to the thoughts of what life could be like if we weren't pastors. In addition to all of this, you must die to the notion that you are enough and begin, instead, to lean on others and let others lean on you. That's where we're going together in this book. The kingdom-minded pastor is willing to be vulnerable, honest, and open to godly correction and encouragement from others, especially other pastors. The kingdom of God is vast. Its operations are not like the world's. The King of our kingdom is superior to all kings and rulers. He is superior in power, authority, love, servanthood, and faithfulness, and humbler than all. This changes so much! I know that you have wishes and dreams for your ministry. I know that your congregation is often begging for your attention. The needs of your flock can consume your mind. It is because of these things that we need to lean into the heart and mind of our King. In your desire to humbly serve and die to self, and in that way emulating Christ, may your soul and your ministry strengthen like never before.

Questions for Further Consideration:

1. What about your current vision for the church might need to change based on this chapter?

2. How does the mustard seed parable of the kingdom encourage you in your ministry right now?

3. In what ways might a kingdom-minded pastors' fellowship catalyze a kingdom movement in your community?

The Isaac Case Coalition has helped me appreciate the breadth of what God is doing in our region through other pastors and local churches. It has also been encouraging to see the level of theological depth being developed among pastors and church leaders.

Jim Culbertson
New England Bible College, Maine
Member of the Isaac Case Coalition

3

Bringing People to the Table

Envision What Could Be

We will begin to get very practical at this point, but I also want you to dream a little. Envision a large table surrounded by likeminded pastors. It doesn't necessarily need to be a table, but let's begin there. The reason you are with this theoretical group of brothers is for intentional kingdom purposes. You all want to accomplish something bigger than yourselves. This is a big deal! Do not take this for granted. Many in our world cannot do this so freely. There are millions of Christians around the world who risk their lives to gather for worship on a Sunday, let alone attempt to gather in a restaurant, office, or public building. Since a meeting of this nature is such a privilege, not one moment of it should be wasted.

As you envision that table, think about the kind of pastors you want there with you. Better yet, who do you need in your life that will help your soul to be healthy, which in turn will affect your home, and your local church? There are criteria to consider, and chapters one and two helped to set the stage for this. You want the men you invite to the table to be of the same mind and heart regarding the essentials. It's very likely that you already know a handful of pastors in your community that fit the criteria. What if you don't? There's a good chance that there is already a pastors' group meeting in your city. Should you just join that one? Let's look at some additional ideas that will help you answer these questions.

Formation

I imagine that many of you are going to need to start from scratch. Truthfully, this might be the better option. It's certainly more enjoyable. When I decided to form a coalition of likeminded pastors in my community (coalition is what I prefer to call it), I started with the men I already knew. Some of them were relationships that had already been formed in other groups, or at conferences, and through common acquaintances. I even met some of them through social media before ever connecting in person. Social media is an excellent way to initiate conversations like this. You can search out local churches, investigate websites, and send a message to initiate a conversation with a pastor. I knew what I wanted in my group: a group of men who were likeminded, and kingdom-minded.

Here's my recommendation at this point. Take a day, sit down, and send out a few emails to local pastors in your area. I did this a lot when I was planting New City back in 2017. I didn't know anyone yet, and I knew that would need to change. A simple, well-written email can turn into an opportunity to grab a coffee. Pray for discernment when you do meet up. Be friendly and kind but be sure to be very clear about your intentions. It's better to be bold with your biblical convictions. Don't hide them, and do not be arrogant. Convey what you're trying to do in a humble manner. Humility is a key component at this stage, whether you're joining an existing group or trying to start a fresh one. I can't repeat that enough. I recognize that no one sees eye to eye on absolutely everything. Methodology can differ among churches even within the same tribe or denomination. So, a humble spirit will help you learn from others and position you to be used by God. You are a pastor, which means God has given you some wisdom and experiences to bring to the table. Let's not ruin the opportunity with pride before a group is formed.

Every Group Will Be Unique

I started our local coalition about a year prior to writing this. It's called the Isaac Case Coalition (ICC). Isaac Case was a reformer in my state in the late 1700s. His work and influence as a kingdom-minded church planter inspired me. I'll share more about him in the final chapter.

I knew that I wanted the Isaac Case Coalition to be more on the reformed side of theology. I wanted it to have at least some level of appreciation for the historical Christian confessions of the faith, because those are my convictions. This may not be the case for you. That's ok. When forming or joining a group with the kind of kingdom impact a pastors' coalition should have, some questions need to be asked. You need to determine how your group can be the most productive in the areas of good fellowship and real encouragement. You can achieve both by seeking biblical unity, but biblical unity is not the same as uniformity. Not all groups need to look alike.

Let's be honest here. Would it be effective to form a group with Wesleyan and Calvinist pastors? Sure, a group like this could be fun and interesting, but it would not be a healthy long-term partnership. You could say the same about a group of charismatic-leaning pastors and traditional Baptists. Groups with this kind of mixture serve good purposes. If the purpose is to pray, eat good food, and plan community events, less alignment is necessary.

Here's an example. We recently had a mass shooting in a neighboring community. Several people died, and the city was broken. In the days that followed, there were gatherings that took place among church leaders and families. Sometimes, there were up to a dozen different church pastors present. I'm sure they had their theological differences and leanings. None of this would have been a good reason not to come together under these circumstances. This level of partnership was good and glorifying to God. It accomplished something special for a unique time. As the dust settled from the tragic event, it was unlikely that these pastors and leaders would go on to plant churches together. The pastors in that community (those truly born-again) are united in faith. This is a strong bond that matters for the kingdom.

So, when I say that each group will be unique, I have two kinds of uniqueness in mind. Firstly, no two groups will be entirely alike simply because the personalities within the group are unique. This is wonderful, and I do not think this needs to be explained further. Secondly, there are more general differences that come from theological bents and convictions held by the group members. Reformed groups and non-reformed groups will have some obvious disagreements and differences. Both groups, operating independently and with a kingdom-mindset, can be effective at forming and encouraging healthy pastors. One group may be more relaxed on the issue of alignment, if no Scripture or primary doctrine is compromised. This is totally fine. For instance, the ICC is made up of primarily reformed pastors, but we have a couple of pastors in the group who are less so. We still desire their fellowship. We want all kingdom-minded pastors to benefit from the group. If done with an attitude of grace, and not a my-theology-is-better kind of attitude, I believe these types of divisions can glorify Christ.

More About Alignment
There are currently a very low percentage of pastors in my town who would align with my philosophy of

ministry, or the essentials of what I believe a biblical church is. There's misalignment, but it's important to realize that not all misalignment is because of sin or outright heresy. Some are good. I admit that there are churches in my state that I don't fully align with, but God is using them for the work of His kingdom. Denying this would be an error on my part. But if a coalition of pastors is going to be effective for the kingdom, alignment needs to be intentional. The criteria for aligning with a group of pastors needs to be stricter than, "God is using their ministry". I'm not an advocate for schisms in the church. I want to be wise. If things happen the right way, then these are people you will be spending a decent amount of time with. Let's say it's once a month for two hours. With too much misalignment in some areas you will end up spending your time arguing and wasting time. What is a biblical church? Are the Scriptures infallible? Does God elect people for salvation before they are born? Should we be ordaining women as pastors? These are just a few examples of doctrinal points which ought to be considered as this sort of coalition is formed. If you want to debate these topics, I recommend doing so in another setting. Healthy partnerships between kingdom-minded pastors requires intentional alignment.

A Few More Things to Discern
If there's already a group of pastors meeting in your area the best way to determine its health is to plan a visit. The goal is to investigate to see if it's right for

you and to see if it is a kingdom-minded group. It's possible that God could lead you to a group of pastors in your area who are already doing the things that this book recommends, a group that will benefit your soul as a pastor and the health of your church. Here are a few assessment questions you can keep in the back of your mind.

1. Is there a love for the gospel
It should go without saying, but the gospel needs to be of first importance. To determine if this already exists in the group, you may choose a well-known confession or creed and ask the group their thoughts on it. The Five Solas of the Reformation could do the trick. You could simply ask "So, what do you brothers think of the Five Solas of the reformation as a summary of the gospel?" If nothing else, you'll have a good debate on your hands. If you already know who will be at the meeting, and the churches they pastor, you might save some time by looking at their website or social media pages. Doing this ahead of time will help you not to waste your time, or theirs for that matter.

2. What kind of conversations dominate the group?
If you do end up visiting a group in your area, discern whether the conversations are intentional for spiritual growth and kingdom purposes. If it is like many of the groups that I've experienced in the past, you'll hear a mix of topics from how everyone's church is doing, discussions about the weather, and the latest win by a favorite team. None of these are necessarily bad

topics, but if these groups are not intentionally gospel centered and aimed at the soul, they will waver and become nothing more than a waste of time.

3. Leadership and submission to Scripture

When you visit your group for the first time, you need to discern humbly whether there is already some established leadership providing direction to the group. A group without leadership will have a hard time serving other leaders well. It shouldn't be hard to find out if the group has a brother or two at the helm who is, himself, a faithful shepherd of a local church.

Another important area to discern is whether there is a collective interest in the truth and in the inerrancy of Scripture. The reason I mention this again here is because this is primarily what will determine if the direction of the group will be good for you and other pastors. You'll want to be a part of a group that submits to the authority of Scripture, not the opinions of man. If you settle for something less, the group will hinder you more than help you. If Scripture is not the foundation, there will inevitably be a lack of biblical and missional focus. Conversations will be weak, and even worse, often sinful and compromising. Having good leadership and submission to the authority of the Bible will protect you and others from the ever-wavering doctrines of the world that creep into local churches every day.

4. Is sin a taboo topic?

Pastors often do not want to be seen as weak and frail, so sin is the last topic to be discussed in a group setting. You are not immune. You need a safe place to lean on brothers for accountability when sin and temptation come knocking at your door. You can't afford for this to be a taboo topic among those you fellowship with. Often, the men who will come to a pastors' meeting do not have a group of godly elders or older men in their own churches to fill this important accountability role. A good coalition can fill this gap and be a life saver. Envision being part of a group that understands that pastors have weaknesses, where matters of sin and failure can be addressed in such a way that you are being called to repentance and faith in the gospel. While there is much more that can be said on this topic, for now, understand that in an age of great compromise in much of the American church, you need men in your life who will call you to account when needed, as well as preemptively drive you to the grace of the gospel.

5. Are there pastors with passion?

Another area to evaluate is the passion of the pastors in the group. I have met pastors who seem to have no passion for their work at all. Passionless pastors will drag you down. I'm not talking about a manufactured zeal that feels fake, or men filled with hot air about themselves. I'm talking about real passion for Christ, passion for preaching His gospel, passion for the transformative work of God's Word in their lives and the lives of the people they lead. I need this in my life. How likely are you to be successful in life and ministry if the people who surround you speak and act as though Christ was not raised from death? Everyone struggles with low days and deep valleys. No one is required to always have a smile on their face. There is even something healthy about lamenting with others through hard times and looking to the gospel together. It is precisely because of the gospel that we do not mourn like the world does. A group of pastors should know better than most that there is joy to be had in every season by looking to who Christ is and what He has done.

Consider this text of Scripture in Matthew 6:21, "For where your treasure is, there your heart will be also." This means that pursuing the things of Heaven is like pursuing a treasure. When you discover a great treasure you run for it, chase after it, and do everything that is necessary to lay hold of it. A person who speaks with passion about a particular subject reveals what they truly treasure. Where is your treasure, brothers? Do not let it be the things of this world, but the things of Christ. If you're going to add one more regular meeting to your schedule, don't settle for something that won't fill you up, encourage your soul, and spur you on in Christ. The kind of men I need fellowship with are those who see the treasure of the kingdom and are running hard after it. We all have differing personality types. Some are generally happy and joyful. Others are slower to express emotion. But what good reason could a pastor have for lacking passion for Christ, His word, and His people? Evaluate the passion of the group. Evaluate your own passion too.

Varying Levels of Experience

You could be reading this as a seasoned pastor in a town that you've been ministering in for years. If this is the case, many would consider you the veteran. It's hard not to see everyone else as the "new kids on the block". Are you able to open yourself up to the kind of group I'm describing? Don't let old prejudices stop you from being part of a good coalition of pastors. This could be the very thing that will help you stay healthy and result in dozens of other men remaining faithful into their later years. Brother, you have so much to offer in terms of wisdom and experience to younger men. Additionally, (and this can be harder to admit) you need to consider how much a younger brother could encourage you in this season. Remember what Paul told Timothy: "Let no one despise you for your youth, but set the believers an example in speech, in conduct, in love, in faith, in purity" (1 Tim. 4:12). It's bad enough when someone in the church despises someone for their youth. When pastors do it to other pastors, it degrades the office. The energy and passion of a young pastor could help to reignite a love for the church that has been lacking in your life.

If you are that younger pastor, or the one who is new to the ministry, here are a few words for you. You have a lot to learn. This doesn't mean you have nothing to offer just because you are new. On the contrary, you have so much to offer. Stay humble, teachable, and glued to the Scriptures. It's often the younger men who are planting new churches, coming into cities and towns like a blaze of gospel glory and expecting to change the world. Keep this zeal but check it constantly. Read books written by both bygone pastors and faithful pastors who are still around. Surround yourself with wisdom and apply what you learn. You are needed, but you are part of a much bigger picture.

Maybe you're reading this, and you are somewhere in the middle of these two scenarios. The church that you pastor is on the small side. You have been there for a few years trying to be faithful to your calling, but the changes you need to make are moving incredibly slowly. You were called there to revitalize something that was declining, but you're not even sure if some of the members are born again. The days are long, and the soil is hard. Nonetheless, there are men in your community right now who could speak into your life and hold your arms up when they get tired. Be patient and persevere. Apply the practical advice of this book and pray for the Spirit to do the work.

Whether I've described your exact situation or not, if you're a kingdom-minded pastor then there is a part of you that craves what I'm telling you. Young, old, new, or veteran, the kingdom-minded pastor knows he needs help, friendship, encouragement, and partnership in the gospel.

Some Highly Practical Tips to Consider:

1. Do some research online, send out emails, prayer-walk in your neighborhood, and connect

for coffee with potential members of the new group. At some point you just need to begin meeting pastors. Compile a list of names that you think you most closely align with. Then, take a step of faith, set a date, and have your first meeting. There will be time to work out the kinks and details as you move forward. Take this important step and meet some pastors.

2. The location of your meeting matters. You could meet at a church office, coffee shop, restaurant, or someone's living room. Wherever you choose, it will need to be conducive to good conversation and allow you to connect without disrupting others too much. The Isaac Case Coalition has met at a local restaurant from 8am to 10am for the last year. The Lord has begun to shape our coalition into something special. We have prayed together, learned from one another, and found encouragement. As with most things, it takes time to develop something meaningful and clear. The commitment levels vary, but a core group is coming into view. The future of this group's health and kingdom fruitfulness will depend in large part on applying the things I'm sharing in this book. Even as I type this, I'm thinking of changes that I believe will be helpful for our coalition. Sharing a meal at a local restaurant has been special and fun, but I believe we can have a more meaningful time in a quieter and more private space. So, we are beginning to meet at one of our group member's

churches and have chosen three others to share in a rotation throughout the year. This will break up some monotony, keep things interesting, and allow those who live in different areas to have less driving some of the time. You will need to determine all of this for yourselves through prayer. Be intentional.

3. How big should the group be? That's going to vary. The size of the space you meet in, the culture of the group, and the goals of the group will all be factors. Don't be too concerned with the size of the group right now. It will likely fluctuate in the beginning as pastors figure out their level of commitment, and as leadership figures out how to communicate the vision of the coalition. Our group has about fifteen pastors in it, with an average of eight to ten who participate monthly. We've had as few as five, and as many as eighteen attend a meeting. It will fluctuate. It will also become steadier over time, Lord willing.

4. At some point you will need to figure out a criterion for joining the group. This can be difficult because it means that there will be some men who will not join based on doctrinal or philosophical differences. As mentioned earlier in the section on alignment, remember that this is okay. Clearly, spelling out the criteria for becoming a member of the coalition will make the group stronger in the long run.

Let me share some examples of the kind of criteria you may want to mention on the front end: first, a member of this coalition must be a lead pastor; second, a member of this coalition must agree with and sign our statement of faith; third, a member of this coalition must agree to the *Chicago Statement on Biblical Inerrancy*. You get the picture.

Once you have met a few times, you will likely develop a friendship with someone in the group to help you work through some of these items. For me, it's a fellow elder with whom I already align very closely. Get together and pray about a plan for onboarding members, faith statements, and other criteria. Be patient and seek clarity. The group will appreciate clarity. Creating a document for the coalition that states theological viewpoints, creeds, and distinctives are all good and have their place. Even if you choose to keep it informal, be sure to be prayerful. Set these things before the Lord. He will lead you.

All of this is meant to be a guide. I cannot tell you exactly what your group should look like but am trying to help build the framework. The concept is sound and is not only possible to do, but crucial for both the kingdom and for your spiritual health. It matters who you "bring to the table". It matters the attitude in which you express the specifics of your group. It matters that you surround yourself with the kind of pastors that will strengthen and hold up your arms when they are weak and weary. Enjoy the process of the early days of your new group. Come back to this chapter for some helpful reminders when you get discouraged. I'm praying for you.

Questions for Further Consideration:

1. What is one thing you can do this week to connect with a pastor in your community in a more intentional and meaningful way?

2. What do you consider to be the most essential criteria to put forward when building a new coalition of pastors?

3. Is passion in ministry something you struggle with, and what can you do to grow in this area?

4. Think of and celebrate a time when you learned something important for your ministry from another local pastor.

4

HEALTHY LEADERS AND
HEALTHY CHURCHES

A pastors' coalition is slightly different than a network. It's less about the local church, and more about the local pastor. Let's talk about what your coalition will do to make you a healthier pastor, and as a result, strengthen the church. If all of this doesn't produce health in your soul, then what good is any of it?

The Discussion
Gathering regularly with doctrinally aligned pastors in my region has allowed us to discuss topics that are relevant to our calling. When I see pastors who are crippled with burdens, it is often because they do not have a solid support system of brothers within

their own church family. Without this, who are they discussing their struggles and joys with? Even a pastor who serves on a team of other pastors is rarely able to discuss his true needs in a vulnerable way that leads to growth. This should not be the case, but it often is. The soul needs good discussion. The pastor's soul needs time and space to process ministry and life issues in a safe environment. The bottom line is that pastors need other pastors, and one of the best ways to build these relationships is in your coalition. It is in this kingdom-minded environment that kingdom topics can be brought to the surface, strengthen the soul, and make you a better leader.

Make a Plan

Plan to discuss topics in your group that are relevant and helpful. Someone will need to plan this out. Select topics of particular interest to pastors and the work of the kingdom. Discussing becoming better preachers, sermon prep, pastoral disciplines, and counseling practices are all interesting to pastors who care about their work. Working through theological points found in confessions and catechisms can be a sharpening endeavor. As mentioned in chapter one, this would be a huge step up from the group that only discusses sports, weather, and complains about their churches and marriages. A carefully chosen theological discussion between a coalition of likeminded pastors could change a man. It could rescue a lonely pastor from the brink of burnout. If we're honest, one of the reasons pastors enjoy group-style discussions is because it allows us to share what we know. We all enjoy strutting just a little. We need to be careful with this because pride is a killer of all good things.

Beyond these common topics, there are many crucial things that can be discussed that are often overlooked. Consider the topic of a pastor's soul. How does a pastor give regular care to his own soul? I agree with Brian Croft and Jim Savastio in their helpful book, *The Pastor's Soul*. Listen to how they describe the importance of soul care.

> While a man is not to obsess over himself, he is to be aware of who he is, how he is doing, and why. He ought to know the state of his own soul. He ought to have some means of gauging his walk with Christ, his integrity, and his heart toward others.[*]

Many pastors have not been taught the importance of soul care. Never once did I hear the phrase until recently and I've been walking with Christ and serving in pastoral ministries for over twenty years. Jesus invites the weak and weary to come to Him and find rest. This means there is even an expectation that His followers, including pastors, will feel weaknesses and weariness. Envision a discussion on soul care taking place in the context of a group of pastors. Undoubtedly, this would be a fruitful topic. If you've been in circles that teach that pastors should never be weak, it's time to abandon that false understanding. In a time when the media is

---

[*] Brian Croft and Jim Savastio, *The Pastor's Soul: The Call and Care of an Undershepherd* (Darlington: Evangelical Press, 2018), p. 6.

filled with pastoral failure, suicide, and burnout, soul care needs to be a prominent conversation. This will be a launching point into other helpful conversations. I like presenting topics to our coalition in question form. Consider these examples, and plan to discuss one of them soon:

- What do you personally do to stay focused on Christ each day?
- What are some of your own personal devotional and worship disciplines?
- When you are weak and overwhelmed, how do you find strength again?
- What failure have you faced this year, and how has God brought you through?

Here are a few more questions that can be asked and discussed, all of which affect the soul and health of a person. Handle with care. Go to a meeting with a willingness to repent from your own sin and trust the gospel.

- Is your family spiritually healthy?
- What can you do to strengthen the spiritual disciplines in your home?
- What are you doing to point your wife to Christ each day?

As the topic is presented and the discussion begins, always be intentional to carry the discussion to a place where true repentance and change can happen. This is where the group really can take a meaningful shape. Another helpful thing can be a few follow-up questions to build on the original. Someone in the group could respond that his family or wife is not doing well spiritually. Follow up with, "Why do you believe your wife is not doing well spiritually?" If it is because of neglect, even unintentionally, this is the opportunity to openly discuss ways that a godly husband should minister to his wife and wash her with the water of the Word. Confess weaknesses and lean on the strength that God has given. Consider these options, all of which are helpful for the soul.

- Is there something particularly difficult about this season of your life and ministry?
- How are you sleeping at night, and what do you do when your soul is restless?
- Are you struggling in your heart to forgive someone?

It's comforting to know that you don't have to deal with any of these serious issues by yourself. Bring them to the middle of a group of men you trust, who share your desire to grow, and who love the kingdom of God. Bring all of these to the Lord in prayer together, and watch God build your coalition into something that honors the King.

Some Personal Examples

When the ICC gathers, we like to get practical. We've talked about study and prayer disciplines, finances, servant leadership, church membership, how to love our families well, tools for discipleship in the church, etc. There are endless topics. Let me share one example of a topic that was timely and meaningful. Maybe it will prove helpful for you.

We had our monthly meeting on a recent Saturday. Ten pastors were in attendance. This is a good number. It was a mix of interns, full time lead-pastors, and bi-vocational pastors. We rarely have everyone in attendance (our WhatsApp chat has over 20 members), but for our rural area, getting ten like-minded leaders in the same room on a Saturday morning is a work of God. I had given some consideration to a recent elder's meeting in my church where we discussed whether the women in our church were being pastored well. It was apparent that the New City Church elder team needed this conversation. We identified a need, and the steps to grow and make it better. I figured that this was not an issue uncommon to other churches, but I wanted to test it out. I decided to make this our topic for that Saturday. Over the course of an hour everyone had the chance to participate. The variety of ages, experiences, and circumstances in the room led to a lot of wisdom being shared and gleaned. One of the older pastors in our group had recently moved from a larger church in New Jersey to a smaller church here in Maine. His congregation is mostly older, which means he does not have the same challenges as many of the newer churches with younger families. His input was gold. Another pastor opened the Scriptures and shared a few things that came to mind while listening to the first brother. The Word was opened, which aligned our thinking with the truth of God's Word. It was a beautiful moment of encouragement and learning. A few of the men confessed ways in which they have struggled to minister to the women in their churches.

When was the last time you sat around a table with a group of pastors who openly admitted their shortcomings? When was the last time you witnessed a genuine sincerity to grow and be a better pastor? This is what was happening in the room that day. It was glorious! When Monday came, I posted a follow-up question in our group chat. I wanted to find out if what was learned in the discussion on Saturday had affected anything on Sunday. One of the pastors had several good conversations with his wife, his daughter, and a few other ladies in the church about the topic of shepherding women. He reported that Saturday's discussion was timely and useful. We all learned and grew closer to one another in the process. The local church benefited. Praise the Lord!

Disagreeing

There will be topics that not everyone sees eye to eye on. Even like-minded pastors can have differing opinions, and that's ok. One of these for our group is church membership. Like the discussion on shepherding the women in our churches well, our discussion on membership allowed us to learn from one another. We all shared success stories, as well as mistakes that we have made. We gleaned wisdom from the Scriptures. When we came to a point of disagreement, unity prevailed, and nothing was derailed. I owe this to the fact that we were already aligned and shared a kingdom heart. Our shared vision, love for the church, and respect for one another was of greater value than being right on this topic. Disagreements can be uncomfortable in any situation. Learning to disagree while remaining in a spirit of brotherly love and unity is possible, and will strengthen you and your local church.

Do Pastors Really Need to Discuss That?

A healthy coalition of pastors will have a strong backbone. You need to be able to discuss issues of a physical nature as well. Many of these have the potential to be more divisive than many spiritual conversations. Consider this example. How well do we rest, exercise, and care for the bodies that God has called us to steward for His glory? A quick observation will reveal that pastors, especially those in full time ministry, struggle to stay in shape. I'm not suggesting that pastors should be lifting heavy weights or running miles a day. I'm not espousing the idea that pastors should look a certain way or be physically stronger than other people. Vanity is a sin for all people. I'm suggesting that if pastors are called to be examples to other believers, especially their own local flock, this should include their physical health as well. If you've struggled in this area, please listen to me. There's so much grace here for you, but don't go too easy on yourself. People are looking to you. Your family is looking to you. Young men are following your lead.

Your physical health can determine if you are able to stay around for those you love, go places God calls you to go, have the energy to serve for years to come. God already has your days numbered. Nothing can thwart His decrees. But these truths are no excuse to ignore wisdom and common sense.

What does this have to do with being a kingdom-minded pastor or being part of a coalition? Let me show you. Staying healthy and in shape takes discipline. When you have nobody to keep you in check, the difficulty increases. You need accountability to keep you going when everything is stacked against you. Brother, you know what it is like to work every day and bear the burdens of others. That's what good pastors do every day. There is no other job on earth quite like it. Dozens, potentially hundreds of individuals and families are depending on their pastors to guide them, lead them, and walk with them through the most difficult situations that life can dish up. There's the weekly sermon that must be prepared, the brother in the church that needs to be discipled through serious sin, and the couple in the church whose marriage is slipping away fast. They are all depending on the loving and careful counsel of a pastor to help them through it. Oh, and moreover, don't forget to eat, exercise, and rest well. See the issue?

This is why in the coming months I plan to bring this topic of health and exercise before the guys in the ICC. I cannot think of a better group to talk about this with. This will provide an opportunity for transparency and accountability, for challenging each other and praying for one another. I wonder how much joy and passion is robbed from the life of a pastor in the long run because his eating and exercise choices do not allow him the energy and stamina to do what he wants to do. You could probably think of other topics that would seem on the surface to be less crucial for the church, but in a group of like-minded men could yield great benefits.

Far-Reaching Benefits for the Church

The kingdom-minded pastor is not centered on his feelings. He has a desire to bless others and lead his congregation. He is an example. Joining and committing to a coalition of pastors says something to the people you shepherd. You are admitting that ministry is not just about you but includes churches and pastors who are laboring around you. As you commit to these brothers you will grow as a shepherd, and your church will feel the benefits. The discussions you have and the trainings you take part in will sharpen you as a preacher and counselor. Learning to disagree well and address hard topics will make you a better communicator. Hearing and learning from the successes and mistakes of other pastors will strengthen you and help to equip you for future trials in the church. Think about the effects that all of this will have on your church members and fellow leaders. They will appreciate you for exposing them to the spiritual blessings of fellowship and accountability among other pastors. You're not just doing this for you, but for all of the people you love.

Questions for Further Consideration:

1. What topics do you think would be good to discuss among a group of doctrinally-aligned pastors?

2. How could partnering with kingdom-minded pastors help you take better care of your soul?

3. Why is it especially beneficial for you as a pastor to discuss hard topics with your coalition?

The Isaac Case Coalition has been a great encouragement to myself, in so many ways. Whether it is the sharpening of our minds, the compassionate sharing of burdens or the joy of hearing what God is doing in other churches, this coalition has been fantastic.

Dan Church
South Lewiston Baptist Church, Lewiston, Maine
Member of the Isaac Case Coalition

5

A KINGDOM-MINDED MISSION

Every church is living out a mission. Some missions are kingdom-minded, and others are not. A good mission statement for a church will clearly portray the mission of the King. A good mission statement does not distract from or take away from the Great Commission that Christ has already given to us. It should be intentionally kingdom-minded. The mission statement of the church I pastor is, "Our mission is to make disciples, develop leaders, and plant churches that multiply."

This statement has served to strengthen our church and develop in me the heart I have today for the mission of the church, and for pastors like you. I still have much to learn. I'm on a journey of constantly refining and correcting. I want to share with you what seems to be working, and what God seems to be blessing in our local ministry. It's a singleness of mind and a constant intentional return to the importance of discipleship and multiplying the kingdom. If you can glean anything from what I'm about to share, and apply it to your situation, then praise be to God. Let's break down the New City Church statement and see how it integrates into a local church. Then I'll attempt to bring it all together in the context of a kingdom-minded pastors' coalition.

Make Disciples

When I began my journey as a church planter in November of 2016, I did not have the fully formed convictions about pastoral ministry and the local church that I do today. They were only ideas at that point. I was a frustrated thirty-four year old who had seen two different ministries that I was a part of come to an end in a six-year span. When we arrived in Maine (my home state) to plant a new church, I was completely sure of only a few things. We needed to be a church that made disciples. I wasn't exactly sure how. I did not want to replicate the prevailing model in American churches. It was too attractional for my convictions.

After a season of prayer, some training, and getting to know our new community, the time came to begin gathering a core team for the new church. I put some posts out on social media about our recent move to town (is that cheating?), our mission, and what we believed God was calling us to do. On January 18th of 2017, we gathered in a rented upper room of a local office building. About fifteen people who had seen the social media post showed up. All of them were believers. Some were members of other churches in the area. Some had been members of a church that closed a few years prior to our arrival. This was all fine with me. We needed to start somewhere, and I wanted to find like-minded believers to begin the work with. If I could have changed anything about this scenario, I would rather have been sent out with a team from a sending-church, but God in His providence had other plans.

I had a simple plan. Share the mission. It was straight from His word. I was not going to compromise it. How could that fail? Six o'clock rolled around. After some introduction and a song or two, I opened the bible and gave a brief talk from Acts 2:42. All I wanted was for them to be excited about a new church in town. I wanted them to love the preaching, love the vision, and love the mission. I wanted them to know that it was my intention that we live our lives as a family. This meant being involved in each other's lives, the Scriptures, and the commission that Jesus gave us. Together. Was it too much to expect some excitement from them too? I finished the message; we sang a couple more songs and prayed together. Had I secured a team of kingdom-minded people to begin this new and important mission for Jesus with my family? When we left that evening, I was hopeful. We had some good conversations. All was seemingly good.

A week later we returned to the same upper room ready to pick up where we left off, ready to storm the gates of Hell together. We got there early to prepare the coffee and set out the appropriate number of chairs based on the previous week, fifteen to twenty chairs. We didn't expect, based on my top-notch performance a week earlier, that the crowd would be cut in half. I began to evaluate if I had done something wrong. I had told them that New City Church was not going to be a church for checking spiritual boxes. I shared with them from Scripture what disciple making and discipleship is in a local church context. I shared with them that I believed the gospel needs to be lived out within a loving community, and how we need to be committed to the proclamation of the gospel together. Surely that is not why people didn't come back. Well, it turned out that this is exactly why. I was so discouraged. I learned from conversations later on that many of them disliked the thought of being a church that made disciples. It scared them. I remember one woman staying late after a meeting to talk with me about this. She questioned being able to commit to other Christians. It wasn't because of church-hurt or anything like that. She questioned the need for members of a local church to have genuine relationships with one another that extended beyond a Sunday meeting. She, and others, questioned basic biblical principles like discipleship and members of a local church helping others to discover and follow Christ. Strange. Sad. Disappointing.

An Increase of Zeal

The truth is, this only made me more zealous for the mission at hand. By God's grace I was not completely deflated by this "set-back". God had given me a feel for the spiritual temperature of my city, and it inspired me to dig in deeper and pray for God to work. Fast forward from this moment on and we have seen God turn a small group of individuals into a family on a mission. I was determined always to place the mission front and center for the church to see. For the first year or two the mission statement read, "Make disciples, Build the church, and Renew the city". Then we changed it to what it is today: "Make Disciples, Develop Leaders, and Plant Churches that Multiply." God used the stubbornness of Christians to remind me that the mission of the church is of utmost importance.

Pastors Need to Live It Out

Pastors need to model discipleship for their flock, whether big or small. Harping on discipleship from the pulpit won't bring the changes. People need to see it, and they need to see it from *you*. Now, I know that you are a busy pastor. Be sure that you are busy with the right things. Make it a priority in your weekly schedule to teach, lead, and set an example for your members of what a life of discipleship and disciple making looks like. Whether you are currently developing a core team to plant a new church, or you are pastoring five hundred members, these words apply to you: "teaching them to observe all that I have commanded" (Matt. 28:20a). Church members need to be able to see their own leaders obeying the Great Commission and finding joy in it. A local church consists of followers of Christ who are constantly observing and growing in the commands of Jesus. One of His commands is to preach the good news of the kingdom, and to welcome new believers into the family who have placed their faith in His death, burial, and resurrection. When a person believes this gospel and is saved, they cannot be left to figure things out alone. They need to be taught and shown the way of Christ through His Word. This is the mission that leads to lasting fruitfulness. This is a kingdom-minded mission because it's an ever-expanding mission, reaching further every day into the darkness of this world one new believer at a time, and pastors need to lead the charge.

Obstacles to the Mission

If you are going to be committed to discipleship and disciple making, then you cannot be afraid to cut programs and nix anything that is getting in the way of His mission, even if this results in receiving backlash. God has called you to shepherd His people according to a standard. The standard is revealed in Scripture. The Scriptures are clear about the mission. Make disciples. Whatever it is that is not allowing you to invest your energy into building and modeling discipleship relationships, get rid of those things. The life and longevity of your church is at stake.

Consider the story I told earlier about the first group of people that gathered with my family in that upper room. Had I given in to their desires, I would have compromised the mission of my King. Had I given in, there's a solid chance that we would have seen quicker growth. Maybe we could have tripled our size, had better facilities and more money, but at what cost? None of those generally positive things are worth abandoning the clear mission our Lord has given to His church. Bigger buildings and more money are not always sinful. You just need to get the priorities right and stay focused on the right kingdom. Brothers, do what you need to do to put the mission of Christ front and center. Put it in a statement. Make it clear. Put it on your website. Run around town with a large banner if you must (kidding, of course). Whatever you do, you need to put the Word of God in front of your face, hide it in your heart, and live out what it teaches.

Develop Leaders

The second part of our mission statement is an overflow of the first. As a local body invests in one another with genuine love and obedience to Scripture, that church body grows spiritually. When members are growing in Christ it is only natural that leaders will emerge. I believe pastors should be intentional about discovering and developing members who have matured and desire to lead.

There's a Wrong and a Right Way

Most churches are not intentionally developing leaders. When pastors have no clear or intentional pathway for new leaders, they tend to fall into what I call the "Osmosis" model. This is what I experienced as a young Christian. There are probably young men in your church that are being called into the ministry. Without a clear pathway, they will spend unnecessary years waiting, wondering if you will notice them, or help them, and unsure about what to do next. This was me. There was no intentionality. I figured out that if I read enough books, and get close enough to the right people, I just might gain the maturity, knowledge, and competencies needed to lead others. This is the osmosis model. I'm not a fan. When Jesus decided it was time to pick His first disciples, well, He picked them. He saw them, went to them, and He called them out. He didn't choose the ones the world would choose. He chose a few men to invest His time and energy into over a three-year period. He taught them, walked with them, showed them His personal disciplines, explained things like prayer, fasting, generosity, and so much more. He warned them of pitfalls and temptation. He displayed great patience and kindness under pressure, and He did it all with intentionality. He said, "Follow me". The model of development you deploy in your church should closely resemble the model of our King. The pastor who intentionally develops leaders is seeing the kingdom as greater than his own ability and reach. He sees the need for developing leaders.

The Mission is Generational

Without leaders, the church flounders, and eventually dies. Perhaps you've witnessed it in your own life, or in your own ministry. I believe this is why this discussion matters. This is why leadership development should be a part of every church's mission. And this is why the mission must be generational. There will be people who come after you are gone. Will they find that you left them a baton to carry? The Great Commission commands that we do this. Look back at Matthew 28 again. Jesus was passing the baton to those He had prepared and developed for the work of His kingdom. The mission of disciple making, and teaching others to make more disciples (leadership), had to go on. From generation to generation, the cycle continues.

Paul picked up the discipleship and leadership baton and gave it to Timothy. He writes, "What you have heard from me in the presence of many witnesses entrust to faithful men, who will be able to teach others also" (2 Tim. 2:2). Somebody must start the process. Perhaps somewhere along the line, the baton fumbled in your church or family. You need to pick it up now. Timothy was next in line. He heard the instruction directly from Paul in the letter he received. I'm sure he had heard it many times in person too. Next in this generational line are the "faithful men" in Timothy's life. He would need to choose them wisely, as do we. These are men in Timothy's local church. They are men in the present, and men in the future who will witness the method and manner that first came from Paul. They would eventually pass Paul's and Timothy's instructions down to more faithful men. The process is clear. Now think back for a minute. Whose message and model are being passed through the generations of men in this scenario? It was Christ's. Had Timothy disobeyed and never passed down what Paul had entrusted to Him in the presence of those witnesses, the church would have come to the same tragic ending that many experience in communities across our world. But if we follow this principle faithfully, there should never be a generation that lacks the leaders required to equip and shepherd the church. This command, when obeyed, is sufficient to supply the church with leaders till the return of Christ. One of the reasons why there is a leadership deficiency today is because pastors keep failing or forgetting to do the intentional work of finding faithful men and handing down the message Paul got from Jesus.

The kingdom grows when kingdom people do the work of the King. Disciples make more disciples. New leaders rise to the surface as God calls them. The local church, and the leaders who shepherd them have the responsibility of recognizing these men, teaching them to observe the commands of Christ, and then mobilizing them to continue. This is kingdom work. The King showed us how to do it. Jesus rejects the osmosis model and so should we. I'm all about organic growth, but even organic growth takes tilling, planting, and watering. It takes work. Pastors, we need to be intentional about this if we are going to see an end to the leadership deficiencies that result in church decline. Pray for this, brothers. Do the work of leadership development. It's part of the mission to make disciples. Put it into the fabric of your church's mission.

Plant Churches That Multiply

Not every member at New City Church is thinking about church planting as much as I am. That's to be expected. I've had a front row seat at seeing the good, the bad, and the ugly of starting a church. My calling and experiences have given me a passion that can be difficult for the average person to comprehend. It's not easy, and not everyone is called to it. For this reason, we chose not to place "church planting" at the front of our mission statement, but at the end. If I were to ask a member at my church to tell me what their personal mission is, I would not expect them to say, "plant churches!" I try to ask our church family that question every few months and I receive a mix of responses as the church grows. Some common answers are, "To reach the lost" or "To be salt and light". These are not wrong answers, of course. They are good answers. One of my favorite responses is when a member says it plain and clear: "Our mission is to glorify God by making disciples." YES! That's it! I do not expect the average member of our church to be thinking about methods to develop good preachers or wondering who the next church planter is going to be. Nonetheless, I believe church planting must find its way into the mission of every church family.

When I sit with new members at a next steps class and talk about the mission and vision of the church, it is a joy to say to them that even though they will not all become church-planters, they all get to be a crucial part of the work of multiplication. That's important for everyone to know.

Not Just Planting, But Multiplying

We're not just throwing church planting at the end of our statement because it's the cool thing to do. We really mean it. It says, "plant churches that *multiply*". That's intentionally written that way to remind us that the work must continue. Every believer who embraces the work of making disciples and helping others follow Jesus in their local church becomes a piece of the multiplication puzzle. Pastors need to model, teach, and fold it into the vernacular of the culture. Make it an outflow of the everyday mission of discipleship. I believe it can and should become the norm for church members to expect multiplication in the life of their church.

When it comes to multiplication, let me encourage you not to limit this to the concept of planting new churches. Disciples who disciple others and then teach them to make disciples is also multiplication. Leaders working with members and training them to be leaders is multiplication. Pastors who are prayerfully and intentionally identifying those who are called to start new churches are engaging in the work of multiplication.

The Multiplication Mandate

God worked multiplication into the fabric of creation. He commanded Adam and Eve to "be fruitful and multiply". This would have been a daunting prospect, no doubt. What would it take for two people who had never had children to fill the earth and subdue it? All they could see was multitudes of creatures filling the air, land, and sea. The human race was outnumbered to an unimaginable degree. Yet this was the command of God. God created human beings to bear His image and fill the earth with His glory.

After creating Adam and Eve, He instituted the family unit – a mother and a father united in body and soul. From their loving union, children are brought into the world. Among many good reasons for having children, one clear reason is multiplication. Mom and Dad are to model for their children what the ultimate purpose of life is, not just how to survive, but how to be productive in this world under the authority of a Creator. Future generations must pass the baton, sharing His creation mandate with the others. God designed children to receive what their parents teach them, and to multiply the work. From generation to generation, we see the creation mandate of multiplication perpetuated.

The Enemy and the Savior
The World is usually opposed to God's design. Enemies of Christ are less intentional about the creation mandate. They often want to slow it down and snuff it out due to their hatred for the life that God gives. Soon after the Fall of man, we see God's redemptive plan revealed. Creation itself would be cursed. Life would now be horrendously difficult. The natural world would now work against this good mandate

of God. Frustration and toil would exist in marriage, in the home, and in daily work. It would affect every good thing. The greatest of these frustrations would come from Satan himself. He would oppose the multiplication mandate and deceive the world to do the same. First, He would get Eve to doubt what God had said, then to doubt His goodness. Adam and Eve both ate what was forbidden and failed to worship and serve God supremely. The results were both spiritual and physical, the most devastating being their banishment from the presence of God, a sign of the enmity now between them. The fall of our first parents led to deeply fallen children with a sin nature just like theirs. Why does Satan care whether people multiply and fill the earth? Because He hates life. He hates the purity of new life. The rest of the biblical narrative makes this abundantly clear.

It is in this Genesis account that God promised that a Serpent crusher would come. From Eden to the first Advent of Messiah in the first century, God was faithful to His people. Against all odds, and despite opposition from Satan and sinful man, God fulfilled the promise. The plan crescendos with the arrival of one new life: a baby that would come from a line of people wrought with rebellion and failure. He was born of a virgin, born to crush the Serpent and save His people. He preached the kingdom, conquered death, and brought forth a new covenant promise that would ensure the success of God's mandate forever. Because of Christ's death, burial, and resurrection, sinners can be reconciled to God though faith, and take part in the most important mission ever thought up.

If we're going to be kingdom-minded pastors, then we must embrace this afresh. Every part of your life and ministry should bear the seal of the King's redemptive mission and mandate to multiply. Can you honestly say that you are on a mission to multiply disciples, leaders, and churches? Allow this to get down to the very core of who you are as a man, husband, friend, church member, leader, and pastor.

Start With the Basics

Multipliers are reproducers. They share their lives regularly with others. This includes spiritual disciplines like reading, praying, worship, solitude, fasting, and others. Consider the discipline of Scripture reading. Everyone could stand to do better at this. I know I can. Take this daily discipline, solidify it in your life, and share it with another disciple. Here's how this might play out in your life. Take the way you practice the discipline of Scripture reading and condense it down for someone else. Try it.

1. What time do you read?
2. How long do you read?
3. What questions do you ask yourself?
4. What do you ask God?
5. Do you ever struggle to understand?
6. How do you fight discouragement in reading?

Answer these questions for yourself, write them down, and begin to ask God to reproduce these traits through you into the life of another believer in your church. God will help you do this. That's the beginning of spiritual reproduction. Here's the part that gets me excited. Imagine yourself sitting with the brother you've chosen to disciple. Maybe he's a future leader in your church. This is a time not only to share with him the how and what of spiritual disciplines. It's also your job to teach him the mandate of multiplication, to do what Paul did with Timothy. Literally tell them that you're passing something on that they will have the privilege of passing on to someone else in the future. Give them the vision that you have for them. Tell them that God designed it this way, for faithful men to hand the things of God down to generations of more faithful men. If you look around and you see no faithful men, it's time to start multiplying. All of this takes time. It takes commitment. But because of the intensity of this work, many pastors just avoid it.

Recall the vision that Jesus gave to His disciples on the mountain before His ascension. He told them that there would be multitudes of people from all nations, tribes, and tongues believing the gospel, following Jesus in baptism, growing in the local church, and glorifying His name. That's a big vision. It's a kingdom-minded kind of vision. The fulfillment of this vision and promise is going to come from multiplication. A kingdom-minded pastor must not abandon the vision and mission of the King.

This example I provided of passing on your discipline of reading is just one (still important) example of the larger point I'm making. Every member of your church, including you and your leaders, needs to be a multiplier. Keep in mind that every person in your life is at a different place in their journey of growth. Shepherds need to walk patiently with people through this process, sometimes leading them through major paradigm shifts due to poor discipleship in their past. Missional realignment like this could shock some people. You've heard of the "cage stage" Calvinist. That's the person who first learns of the glorious doctrines of grace and then goes about like a bull in a China closet running people over with this new discovery. Well, try not to be a "cage stage" multiplier. These things take time and intentionality. Do the work, model it faithfully, and God will bring the increase.

What's This Have to Do with Pastors' Coalitions?

Why is all of this in a book about coalitions and partnerships between doctrinally aligned pastors? Let me explain. Take everything that has been brought forth in this chapter and apply it as a shared work with your coalition. Remember when I mentioned that most members are not automatically thinking about multiplication? It's also true that a lot of good, well-intentioned pastors are not yet thinking about it either. Some are so busy and bogged down with maintaining programs and attendance that to even consider church planting might be seen as a hindrance to progress. For some it is only a distant hope, but not a present reality. I get it. You need a healthy foundation. You need to get some things in order first. Yes, do this. Only do not neglect the mandate. I've attempted to make clear that when the multiplication mandate is central to your life and ministry, it will spill over. If you need more leaders in your church, multiply yourself as a leader with the strength that the Spirit supplies. Start with the basics and go from there. If you need more people doing discipleship in your congregation, because right now you're doing most of the work, start sharing the multiplication mandate with a few individuals. Teach them to make disciples. Set the example, pray, and follow up with them to assess and encourage their growth.

A Kingdom-Minded Coalition of Pastors

Keep multiplication a central theme of your new group. This new coalition exists to make you stronger as a pastor. It exists to help other pastors grow in Christ and become better pastors. One of the most exciting aspects of the coalition I'm a part of is when we talk about kingdom work together. Usually, when churches talk about doing projects together it ends up being about outreach, community service, a worship and prayer night, etc. These are not bad things by any means. We need those things. But remember, you don't need a doctrinally-aligned coalition to get together with local churches for a community work project or night of singing. When it comes to multiplying the kingdom through disciple making, leadership development, church planting and revitalizing, however, you need a more unified group, like the one you're working on now, or will be soon.

Your new coalition is the perfect place to regularly ask questions like, "Is there a community near us that lacks a gospel presence?"; "Are there any up-and-coming leaders in our churches that we can work together to develop?"; "Does anyone know of a local church that needs a pastor?" These are questions that lead to movements when the right people are involved. Topics and discussions like these, in addition to the topics mentioned earlier in the book, will help to keep you focused on the mission together. It's easy to get distracted. It's easy to become too focused on the latest world event, or the fires you're putting out. You need to put out "fires", protect sheep, and fend off wolves. It's part of your job as a shepherd. But these tasks do not replace the mandate of multiplication. They're part of it.

The younger pastors in the group will find strength in the conversation about mission and discipleship. It will be encouraging for him to see seasoned pastors who have not lost their focus on the kingdom. The revitalizer in the room will be encouraged by brothers and pastors who are willing to be in his circle with him, give counsel, and help to identify his blind spots. We have a brother in our group right now who for the last year has struggled with a disunified elder team due to theological disagreements. At our last meeting, the subject came up again. We prayed for him and reminded him that he is not alone. We all offered to come alongside him in more practical ways, just being available should he decide he needs us. Many pastors do not have the kind of space needed to talk about hard ministry topics while maintaining a joyful love for the gospel, the ministry, and our sovereign God. The veteran pastor will find his faith being challenged by the freshness and zeal coming from the young church planter or seminary grad. All kinds of pastors will find blessing and benefit in this kingdom-minded coalition.

God is winning. The kingdom is advancing. The church is alive and well. Christians, everywhere, are serving their King. There are pastors everywhere who need to be encouraged to hold on, look to their King, band together, and stay focused on His mission. As I begin to land this plane, I want to leave you with a sense of optimism. I want to draw your attention to two men (there are many more) who displayed remarkable kingdom-mindedness in their day, and whose lives and ministries have inspired me. Let's look back together and see what we can learn.

Questions for Further Consideration:

1. Have you ever seen kingdom-minded multiplication modeled by leaders in a local church? How has that example impacted you negatively, or positively?

2. What is an area of Christian discipline that you can begin to model and multiply in others in your church? How will you do that?

3. What are the biggest items standing in the way of your church developing leaders? How might your coalition help you work through this?

6

LOOKING BACK

It's helpful to measure ideas against history. If it has been tried before, was successful, and produced good fruit, then we should pay attention to it. What I have proposed in this book is not a new concept. Many have seen the fruits of something as practical as pastors partnering together around a kingdom mission. The two men mentioned in this chapter are not unlike us. They had aches and pains. They struggled with besetting sins. They had wives and children to provide for, and churches to shepherd through seasons of blessings and trials. They served in large cities, and in rural communities and colonies. There are several common denominators that led to their effectiveness. Chief among these is the fact that they believed God had inspired the Scriptures, and the gospel was central in their preaching. They faced sadness, ridicule, weakness, and loneliness, all of which threatened their lives. They trusted in the sovereignty of God. Would you believe that something as simple as partnership in the gospel would strengthen these men in their times of need? Kingdom-mindedness affected their ministries and those they served alongside. Doing gospel work with faithful men who shared their convictions and loved the kingdom was both foundational and formational for them. There is so much we can learn from them.

Charles Spurgeon and a Band of Brothers

Those who know me know that I love Spurgeon. He has impacted me like few others have. To be clear, I'm not presenting a full view of his life and ministry in this short chapter. Others have done that.* Not to mention the scores of works written on Spurgeon throughout history. Maybe I'll take on a more extensive Spurgeon project in the future, but for now I'll share just enough to reinforce the premise of our current subject.

In a recent article, Geoff Chang shares how some came to view Spurgeon's associationalism, specifically after the famous Downgrade Controversy. Chang notes, "In retelling the story of the Downgrade Controversy, some have argued that Spurgeon entirely

---

* See, for example: Alex DiPrima, *Spurgeon and the Poor: How the Gospel Compels Christian Social Change* (Reformation Heritage Books, 2023); Ed Romine, *The Booming Baritone Bell of England: The Pedagogy and Practice of Charles Haddon Spurgeon's Open-Air Preaching* (Pickwick, 2023); Geoff Chang, *Spurgeon the Pastor: Recovering a Biblical and Theological Vision for Ministry* (B&H, 2022), just to name a few.

gave up on all formal associations."[*] Spurgeon was indeed wounded by the downgrade. The Baptist Union and other London associations were important to him. He had even hosted and chaired their meetings. What happens when the associations you once loved start to embrace unbiblical doctrine and compromise their core theological convictions? You leave. That's what he did.

> A new religion has been initiated, which is no more Christianity than chalk is cheese; and this religion, being destitute of moral honesty, palms itself off as the old faith with slight improvements, and on this plea usurps pulpits which were erected for gospel preaching. The Atonement is scouted, the inspiration of Scripture is derided, the Holy Spirit is degraded into an influence, the punishment of sin is turned into fiction, and the resurrection into a myth, and yet these enemies of our faith expect us to call them brethren and maintain a confederacy with them![†]

The Fraternity

Spurgeon withdrew on solid grounds in my opinion. The departure from sound doctrine on the part of the Baptist Union was clear. During this season of withdrawal from the Union, something else

---

[*] Geoff Chang, "Spurgeon's Associationalism After the Downgrade Controversy", *The Spurgeon Center*, October 5, 2022, https://www.spurgeon.org/resource-library/articles/spurgeons-associationalism-after-the-downgrade-controversy/.

[†] Chang, "Spurgeon's Associationalism".

emerged. He started his own association. Soon after his departure, he and Archibald Brown formed an informal group of pastors, a fraternity. It began with seven men. They desired the fellowship and unity of likeminded pastors. I propose that there was a kingdom-minded cause behind this new group. According to Chang, "Over time, they would invite other like-minded pastors across all denominations to join their group, so that eventually, 30 pastors belonged to this fraternal."*

The Downgrade Controversy nearly ended associationalism for Spurgeon, but partnership was in his blood. Over time, the thirty pastors who made up the group decided that an informal gathering was not sufficient. It was time to draft a statement of faith, a way to recognize that their shared convictions were not based on a whim, but on the truth of God's Word. A statement of faith would help them to be distinguishable from the compromise that prevailed in London. It had to be clear that the fraternity agreed on the essentials of the gospel. In 1891 this confession was published in an issue of *The Sword and The Trowel*:

We, the undersigned, banded together in Fraternal Union, observing with growing pain and sorrow the loosening hold of many upon the Truths of Revelation, are constrained to avow our firmest belief in the Verbal Inspiration of all Holy Scripture as originally given. To us, the Bible does not merely

---

* Chang, "Spurgeon's Associationalism".

contain the Word of God but is the Word of God. From beginning to end, we accept it, believe it, and continue to preach it. To us, the Old Testament is no less inspired than the New. The Book is an organic whole. Reverence for the New Testament accompanied by skepticism as to the Old appears to us absurd. The two must stand or fall together. We accept Christ's own verdict concerning "Moses and all the prophets" in preference to any of the supposed discoveries of so-called higher criticism.

We hold and maintain the truths generally known as "the doctrines of grace." The Electing Love of God the Father, the Propitiatory and Substitutionary Sacrifice of his Son, Jesus Christ, Regeneration by the Holy Ghost, the Imputation of Christ's Righteousness, the Justification of the sinner (once for all) by faith, his walk in newness of life and growth in grace by the active indwelling of the Holy Ghost, and the Priestly Inter cession of our Lord Jesus, as also the hopeless perdition of all who reject the Savior, according to the words of the Lord in Matt. xxv. 46, "These shall go away into eternal punishment,"—are, in our judgment, revealed and fundamental truths.

Our hope is the Personal Pre-millennial Return of the Lord Jesus in glory.[*]

---

[*] Chang, "Spurgeon's Associationalism".

That's an impressive statement for a group of local pastors. Whether the above statement of confession inspires you or not, let's admit a few things together.

There Will Always be Churches with Compromised Doctrine

This is not a call to hunt for heretics, but to be faithful shepherds over your flock and in your community. Downgrades in denominations (and non-denominational churches) will affect everyone differently. As a pastor, you must remain watchful. Don't be naïve. God may ask you to take a stand like Spurgeon did. Maybe you need to leave an association or network that has become biblically compromised. If so, do so with wisdom and humility, but whatever you do, do not isolate yourself. Take a stand to be faithful to the truth. Like Spurgeon, hold firmly to the doctrine of Sola Scriptura – Scripture as final authority. Spurgeon's story gives us great reason to band together with other like-minded pastors. When compromise abounds, your congregation will look to its leadership. Holding the line is necessary. Holding the line together with others will lighten your load and strengthen your resolve to persevere. Local congregations will be more confident during wavering times knowing that like-minded brothers are banding together to lead their congregations against the tides of compromise.

Be Bold with Doctrinal Clarity

As a pastor, you need to be bold and unashamed. Like Spurgeon and his fraternity, you need to be willing to confess your faith before any number of witnesses. Whether they be peers, community leaders, church members, or in Spurgeon's case, people from within your own tribe or denomination who have swayed from sound doctrine, you need to speak up for what is true. Doctrines such as the sufficiency and exclusivity of Christ, substitutionary atonement, and the inerrancy of Scripture are not minor or tertiary doctrines. These matter to the fabric of what a New Testament church is. Where I live, not all professing Christians and pastors would affirm these equally. When an era is fraught with compromise, the kingdom-minded pastors need to take a stand. Good doctrine is worth defending, clarifying, and proclaiming, so that the people you shepherd and those you seek to reach are discipled in healthy churches.

The need for bold, doctrinal clarity among pastors has not lessened nowadays. Let us learn from the boldness of Spurgeon, and the twenty-nine other men who signed that document. What might this look like for you and the pastors in your region? Start with a conversation in your coalition about what doctrines are worth fighting for, or potentially being ostracized for. What if your group were to draft a document together which highlighted several points of faith that directly opposed some of the mainline denominational views held in your area? More than upsetting a few people, many will thank the Lord for you. Christians in your city will know which pastors and churches are standing upon the Word of God. Your bold doctrinal clarity might stir up trouble with some, but for others it will be a blessing. The church will be encouraged to march on knowing that their leaders are pioneering the way. While we aim for clarity, be sure to maintain the right attitude.

With Pain and Sorrow
It should never be our aim to gloat, or tease, or rub doctrine in the face of anyone. Right doctrine creates humility and gentleness, even if you think you are on the correct side of an argument. When Spurgeon's Fraternity published their statement of faith it was out of a growing pain and sorrow over what they observed. The sin was described as the loosening hold of many upon the truth. When an individual or church begins to loosen their hold upon the truth, this is a time to mourn and stand. Be sorrowful over the error. Be sorrowful over the compromise that is leading others astray. Be sorrowful because the very definition of what it means to be a Christian and believe the Bible is being changed before your eyes. Few seem to care. We are also in pain. It pains us to see deception coming from leaders who claim to speak the truth. Because of this pain we are driven to action.

Because we love the truth, we will hate that which threatens it. How did Jesus correct and rebuke those who claimed to have the truth yet led others astray?

> Whoever receives one such child in my name receives me, but whoever causes one of these little ones who believe in me to sin, it would be better for him to have a great millstone fastened around his neck and to be drowned in the depth of the sea. (Matt. 18:5-6).

Jesus hates deception. He hates when those who claim to follow Him cause His little ones to sin. We must share this hatred. Damage is being done and we cannot sit in silence. How do we stand up? We do not wrestle against flesh and blood. This is not a circumstance that requires physical violence. Remember that we are in a battle for the truth. We stand up against those who lead others astray by knowing, believing, proclaiming, and uniting around what is true in Scripture. Your pastors' coalition will aid you in this very thing. Spurgeon's fight was for the truth. He and his men stood together as soldiers. They put their flag of doctrinal clarity firmly in the ground with God's kingdom authority. May we learn this also and have the boldness to fight for what is true in our communities. Gather the like-minded men. Look to Jesus and His Word for clarity. Write down what you need to be most clear about. Pray and act.

Isaac Case: Associating For Multiplication

I was introduced to Isaac Case a couple of years ago as I was preparing for a conference in my area. An acquaintance of mine heard that I was doing research to find a New England reformer that I could present at the conference and bring encouragement to local under-shepherds. He began sending me articles from church archives he had discovered from towns in my state. These articles and meeting minutes from local churches and Baptist associations were so impressive, so rich with gospel-vitality, so full of revival that I could hardly believe what I was reading. Isaac Case is one of the individuals whose name shines brightly in New England church history. Other than a few articles online, I cannot find any thorough biographical works written on Isaac or his companions. I expect that to change soon. This short section will not do justice to what he deserves. May it bring you encouragement, nonetheless.

Isaac was born in Massachusetts. He was 18 years old when he first trusted in Christ. It was 1779. Life in New England was hard then, harder than today. The streets and highways were mud and dirt. Travel was difficult. Many churches had been planted, but doctrinal fidelity was already compromised with universalism. The sweet doctrines of salvation by grace alone, through faith alone, in Christ alone were not held dear by most who warmed the pews. Hearts were cold like the long winters, but Isaac Case had heard his "Macedonian call", and it could not be resisted.

A church member sent a letter to one of Isaac's associates expressing the spiritual need in Maine and he responded to the Lord in obedience. The years that followed were filled with bold gospel-proclamation that swept through the pine tree state like wildfire. Hearts were consumed with the conviction of sin and faith in the Son of God. Story after story tells of genuine conversion through repentance and faith. As men and women came to faith through the preaching of the Word, believers were assembled into local churches. They constituted and covenanted together for the continued work of the gospel and the regular observance of Christ's ordinances, baptism, and the Lord's Supper. New churches were being planted across the state, not by gimmicks and tricks, but by the ordinary means of God's grace. An incredible thing began to take shape. Isaac and his associates saw the newly formed churches growing in health and strength, and they seized upon an opportunity.

In an 1845 publication entitled, "A History of the Baptists in Maine", Joshua Millet writes,

The three churches before described, increasing in numbers, power and influence, and Baptists rapidly multiplying in the new settlements in every direction around these central points of gospel light, encouraged the belief that the prospect was brightening, that other churches would soon arise to co-operate in the general work of evangelizing the whole State. It was deemed, therefore, not only expedient, but even the duty of these churches, to commence holding annual meetings, in which all the churches might associate, and deliberate upon things relating to their own welfare, and the prosperity of Zion in general. These views, and the feelings of fraternal love and interest which dwelt in the hearts of these early Baptists, originated the ' Bowdoinham Association,' which was organized at the dwelling house of Rev. Job Macomber, in Bowdoinham, on the 24th day of May, 1787.*

Pastors and leaders today need to look at our mission in a similar way to these eighteenth century New England believers. Why did they associate together? According to Miller, they did it for their welfare and the prosperity of Zion in general. Zion is mentioned over 150 times throughout Scripture. Zion begins as a seat of power in Jerusalem after it was captured by David in 2 Samuel. From there, it expands to take on a larger scope, including the temple itself. To the ancient Jews, Zion was about the presence of God, His rule and reign. In the New Testament, the definition of Zion expands even further to take on the spiritual kingdom:

> For it stands in Scripture:
> "Behold, I am laying in Zion a stone,
> a cornerstone chosen and precious,
> and whoever believes in him will not be put to
> shame" (1 Pet. 2:6).

Jesus is the cornerstone of Zion. Believers in Christ are the individual stones that make up the spiritual city which Christ is building. We have no need to be ashamed because our King is the Cornerstone who holds us all together. The prosperity of Zion is the prosperity of the church, whom Jesus purchased with His own blood. To think about the general good of

---

* Joshua Millet, *A History of the Baptists in Maine*, (Portland: Charles Day Co. 1845), 102.

Zion is to think of the general good of all believers, all true gospel ministries, and all kingdom-growth in this dark world.

As these churches in New England were being planted and growing, it became necessary for the overall prosperity of the church that these smaller local churches begin to associate together. Consider the intentionality here. What churches do you know that still associate together for the kingdom? Even more rare is to see healthy associations where there is still doctrinal clarity and fidelity. Working together should not mean compromising the truth but helping each other to become further established in the faith once delivered to the saints. The "prosperity of Zion" is a kingdom-minded motivation, one that should still exist today in each of our ministries.

Another reason why they associated together was to "deliberate on things relating to their own welfare." Whether you are a part of a healthy association or not, I'm sure you can see the merit here. A person's welfare is important. A local church's welfare is also vital. A once-per-year gathering of churches in a small or large region could very well be what encourages a pastor to keep going, hang on, and not throw in the towel. Though this book isn't as much about church-to-church partnerships as it is about pastoral partnership and fellowship, they can often go hand in hand.

When I go to the annual flagship conference of the network my church is a part of, I always leave built up and encouraged in my ministry. The Pillar Network functions as a global network, having grown to almost five hundred churches. In our regions, we function as an informal association of churches and pastors. We seek fellowship around a common set of DNA. We are doctrinally-aligned and missionally-driven. The alignment of our theological convictions helps us to serve Christ together in the starting and strengthening of churches, as well as revitalization. Not all associations are healthy. Some are, but many need help and realignment. Perhaps a reminder from men like Isaac Case would do associational leaders some good.

When these new Maine Baptist ministers began to gather for their welfare, it was genuine, and gospel centered. Millet continues:

> This was a memorable day for the Baptists in this part of the State. Being but few in number, (as the entire number of Baptists represented in this meeting was 183 only,) and in the midst of a rapidly growing population, and an increasing Baptist community, it became important that every measure adopted, every sentiment expressed, and every motive professed, should be according to gospel love, truth, and righteousness ; and that every precedent established should be such as all the churches and Associations which might afterwards arise, could follow with safety and delight.[*]

They came together so that they might deliberate on things relating to their spiritual welfare. They did it with intentionality. They did it annually in a formal

---

[*] Millet, *Baptists in Maine*, 102.

sense, but their fellowship and partnerships carried well beyond the yearly meeting, "that every measure adopted, every sentiment expressed, and every motive professed, should be according to gospel love, truth, and righteousness." Oh, how we need this today in every place where churches exist and are being planted. It is far too often that we see the emphasis of love without truth, or truth without charity, or love without a desire for biblical righteousness.

> In the course of business, the Association adopted a summary of doctrinal articles, which constitute the foundation, yea, which embody the very soul and spirit of the articles of Faith and Covenant now universally adopted by the denomination throughout the state. The document to which we refer reads thus: In associating ourselves we disclaim all pretensions to the least control on the independence of particular churches; our main design is to establish a medium of communication relative to the general state of religion ; — recommend such measures ; — give such advice ; — and, render such assistance as shall be thought most conducive to the advancement, peace and enlargement of the Redeemer's kingdom.[*]

The association of churches drafted and adopted articles to clarify doctrine so that the Redeemer's kingdom might be enlarged in Maine (or any state or region). These adopted articles were not meant to control, but to allow for open accountability among the associating members. A shared confession of faith

---

[*] Millet, *Baptists in Maine*, 102.

and a shared understanding of basic ecclesiology would align their hearts and aid in the strength of the churches. The Lord clearly blessed the association, and He did so amid great opposition:

> It may seem somewhat surprising to the present generation who are accustomed to see the Baptists multiplying so rapidly in these eventful days of enlarged means and wonderful prosperity, that they should make so slow progress at their commencement. But should those who thus wonder, consider the persecutions of some, the trials, the obstacles to success common to all in a new country ; — could they see the minister travelling on foot through the woods, guided only by 'spotted trees,' to get to destitute settlements ; — could they see the scattered settlers, walking six, ten or twelve miles to an evening meeting, or drawn through the unbeaten snow on an ox-sled, seated on a bundle of straw, to the place of worship where they might hear the words of life, the wonder would seem to be, that they multiplied so fast the minister was encouraged to endure hardness as a good soldier, from the success he witnessed ; — and the people were excited to make great exertions to hear such ministers as manifested so much concern for their souls. As the result of such movements, the obstacles notwithstanding, churches continued to increase.[*]

Those who associated together saw the fruits of multiplication. Good churches increased in number. Sinners believed the gospel. Associations were strong

---

[*] Millet, *Baptists in Maine*, 102.

and focused. It was needed in the late eighteenth century, a time when universalist and anti-gospel movements were prevalent. It is needed again in our time. I'm asking the Lord for a movement in my region, and in regions across the country and world that only the Spirit of God can do. We need to pray for it. Let's follow in the steps of these bold men of God.

What I've proposed in the earlier chapters of this book regarding kingdom-minded pastors and coalitions is not unlike what we read of Case, Spurgeon, and others. What would happen if our pastors' coalitions and monthly meetings began to function like these early associations? What if every town and region in your state had like-minded pastors meeting together for the good of Zion in general? What if these associations began to strengthen the frontlines of gospel ministry in a time when truth is being challenged by mainline denominations every day? It is for this reason that I decided to call our group the Isaac Case Coalition. There is a memorial to Isaac Case standing in Manchester, Maine. At the top it reads, "Elder Isaac Case: Patriot – Preacher – Church planter."

Questions for Further Consideration:

1. How does Spurgeon's story encourage you as you think about partnerships with other pastors?

2. What stance could you see yourself taking with other pastors to provide doctrinal clarity for people in your community?

3. How have you found your local associations to be helpful or unhelpful for the cause of the kingdom?

4. What did Isaac Case mean by "For the prosperity of Zion", and how can you apply that to your outlook for ministry?

Conclusion

Thank you for taking this journey with me. Some of you have many years of experience shepherding God's people in the local church. I am sure there are many things I would enjoy sitting and listening to you talk about, things you are passionate about that would strengthen my life. Helping pastors to grow in their calling, to develop their competencies, and to become stronger in their Great Commission focus has been a passion of mine for a long time. God has used past experiences to teach me that good pastors and healthy churches do not just happen automatically; they're developed intentionally.

When I began pastoring full time in 2017, I had a mentor who chose to invest in me the training and the truths that altered the course of my ministry forever. He was a church planting catalyst for the North American Mission Board. Providentially, God put me and a small group of church planters with Barry for a short season to glean some wisdom before starting our new churches. Beyond the required training for Send Network, I grew to love this brother and how he could minister to needs so well. He was gospel-centered and kingdom-minded. He pointed me to Christ in every blessing and every crisis. In a short time, Barry had inspired me to love pastors, and do everything I could to help them grow and thrive.

That's why this book matters to me. That's why you matter to me, brother. I want you to be successful. I want you to persevere. You matter as a pastor because your calling, and that of countless others, abides till Christ returns in glory. Until then, the kingdom needs men like you to hold the line. You'll need to draw some lines as well. When pastors have a deep love for the gospel, a deep love for Jesus, for His church, and for His mission, the local church will be strong and multiply. Add one more layer to that. Many of the problems being faced in the church would diminish if pastors had a deep, genuine, kingdom-minded love for other pastors. When a pastor facing loneliness, anxiety, frustration, and stagnant ministries can get into a room with other pastors who love him and have the spiritual fortitude to hold up his arms in his time of trouble (Exod. 17:11-12), that pastor has a far better chance of avoiding burnout and bearing fruit.

The very first thing I'd like you to do when you finish this book, if you have not done so already, is call a pastor that serves in a church close by. Ask him if he has a group of pastors that he meets with regularly. It's possible that he does. Even if he does, try to find out what the group is doing. Ask him what it means to him to be a kingdom-minded pastor. Once you get an idea from him what it means, I want you to share a few of the principles that have been laid out in this book. Share what it means to be about the Great Commission. Tell of the encouragement you received from the mustard seed parable of the kingdom. See if you can use that to shine hope on a situation. You probably know at least one pastor who is discouraged by the low attendance, the short list of Sunday school volunteers, or the small budget. The mustard seed always starts small but eventually grows into a great tree. That's the way of the kingdom. Ask some helpful questions out of genuine interest for his soul, and then offer to pray for him. Ask him to pray for you. Let him know that you've just read a book about starting local coalitions with doctrinally aligned pastors to help pastors and churches become and stay healthy. If he's uninterested or too busy for another monthly meeting, kindly end the call and seek the Lord for the next step. Eventually, even if it's only one or two, you'll form a group.

Ten years from now, I'd love to see and hear about hundreds of kingdom-minded coalitions, like the Isaac Case Coalition, meeting together and multiplying all over the country. One thing that will result from this is more pastors who think, live, and serve like their King. Having intentionally spent time in the company of brothers who love Jesus and His church like you do, and who genuinely care for your soul, you will grow in your love. You will be sharpened. Your theology will be clearer and warmer. Your ability to teach local church members, elders, and deacons about the importance of kingdom relationships will increase and bear fruit in your own church. Those who know you will be encouraged by your optimism. On top of this, your family will appreciate the sense of strength that is growing in you. Your wife will appreciate that your load is lighter and countenance brighter. Your strength in the Lord will lead to her stability and growth as well. I believe this is a movement worth praying for.

Are you with me?

Enjoy a sample from another Christian Focus and
Practical Shepherding resource:

Pastoral Friendship
The Forgotten Piece to a Persevering Ministry

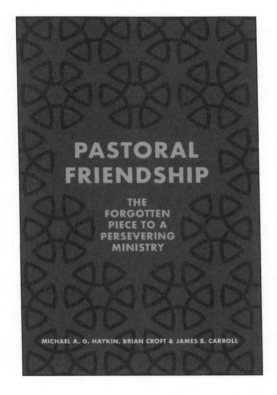

By Michael A. G. Haykin, Brian Croft,
and James B. Carroll

978-1-5271-0916-2

7

Modern Exhortations to Pastoral Friendship

Indeed, J.C. Ryle was correct in noting, 'Friendship halves our troubles and doubles our joy.'* Despite increasing connectedness, many in our culture face a growing isolation of the soul and pastors are prime candidates for this paradoxical lifestyle. But we can't care well for the souls in our congregation if we're weary and wandering ourselves. Even though we interact with dozens of people in our churches and social media circles, we often foster few, if any, spiritual friendships. We hope by now you're convinced that this instrument of grace is vital for personal growth and pastoral longevity and are ready to commit to developing God-glorifying, Christ-exalting, Spirit-empowered friendships for the sake of your soul and those under your care.

The aim of this final chapter is to encourage each pastor to consider how he might pursue his own

---

* J. C. Ryle, *Practical Religion*, (Carlisle, PA: Banner of Truth, 2013), p. 317.

pastoral friendships in the days ahead. We will seek to accomplish this in two ways. First, we will suggest ten exhortations on how pastors might begin to develop meaningful, trusted, and loyal friendships in their own lives. Second, we will share real, personal examples from our own lives on how ministry friendships have been a tremendous blessing, a means for spiritual growth, and have proven to be that forgotten piece to help any pastor persevere in his ministry.

1. Die to self

All three synoptic Gospels record the following famous words from Jesus, 'If anyone would come after me, let him deny himself and take up his cross and follow me.'[*] Selfishness impedes progress in friendship as in all other areas of spiritual growth. While we don't die for others in the way Jesus did, each of us must be prepared to 'lay down his life for his friends.'[†]

Brian: My good friend, Jim, shares a birthday with my youngest daughter. On her fifth birthday this busy pastor who lives across town showed up at my house on his birthday to bring her six specialty cupcakes from Gigi's cupcakes. My daughter got to determine which cupcake she wanted and who of our family of six got one of the other Cupcakes. As you can imagine, my friend made a lifelong friend with my daughter that day, known for many years to come as, 'Her birthday

---

[*] Matthew 16:24; Mark 8:34; Luke 9:23.

[†] John 15:13.

buddy!' My friend repeated this very selfless act for several years to come. This busy pastor, with his own birthday to celebrate and his own flock to care for, showed up at my front door out of love for me and my daughter for the next five plus years.

Many times, dying to self in pastoral friendship is not about some loud, dramatic sacrifice, but best illustrated by a small, thoughtful, unexpected, and intentional act of kindness. Every pastor knows one of the best ways to love a pastor is to love his family. In loving my daughter in this unique way, I felt his love for me. On my daughter's thirteenth birthday the tide turned. She showed up at Jim's church on a Wednesday night with a box full of Gigi's cupcakes, a sweet gesture of how much Jim's birthday visits had meant to her—and to me.

2. Invest wisely in relationships

Passivity rarely produces anything of value, but equal investments also rarely yield identical returns. Prepare for the work of befriending and pray for discernment concerning where to apply it. Not every potential friend will reciprocate and often the truest ones will come in surprising places.

Michael: Friendships take time and energy. Over the years, I have carved out time to invest in friendships, most of which have developed from a teacher-student relationship. What this has meant is purposefully contacting these friends and spending time in person with them or speaking to them over the phone or now by Zoom. I am deeply invested as an academic and it would have been easy for me to have spent this time in academic pursuits. But I knew that I needed friendships for the good of my soul. I had seen the dangers of ignoring such a need in the life of my own father, who, too, was a lifelong academic. In his case his field of study was electrical engineering. He was so focused on his vocation that he had no real time for friends. I was determined not to be like that.

3. Value the power of presence

Most people assume friendship is about a relationship with someone that is based on interactions, conversations, advice, wrestling through struggles, and talking through solutions. This is certainly assumed in pastoral friendships as we seek relationships with other pastors to help us wade through the tricky waters of pastoral ministry. But sometimes what we need is a friend who is willing to simply sit with us in silence, be present, and listen. There is a value in the power of presence when a human being sits with another human being to be a warm, accepting, and loving presence who listens.

Brian: One of the most important friendships in my life is with a fellow pastor—we meet for a coffee every Wednesday morning. The sole focus of this time together is to care for one another's soul. We rarely talk about ministry problems. We don't hash out solutions to church challenges. We don't discuss our sermon series we are preaching. We talk about each other. We check in on our emotional state, mental capacity, and spiritual engagement. Nothing is off limits. We can bring whatever we need to bring to each other and there is no judgment. We come together to assess the activity of our own souls before God. We best accomplish this through a single commitment to one another—presence. We are committed to come together and simply sit with one another. Sometimes one of us shares more than the other. But our commitment is to sit and listen and be present to the need of the other.

Sometimes our most meaningful friendships are not those relationships where we come together to dialogue, but those relationships that invite sitting together in silence and simply enjoying the presence of the other. That's what this friend is to me. And it is special. With the number of voices in a pastor's life, I assume all pastors would be better equipped to persevere in ministry if they had friendships that had less words and more warm presence as its foundation.

4. Seek friendships inside and outside the church and lead your wife to do the same

While the value of friends in the same ministry trench cannot be overstated, the addition of friends outside our particular ministry field is also important. Time and distance make these relationships more difficult to develop and maintain, but they sustain a pastor and his wife in unique and critical ways.

Brian: Some of my most meaningful pastoral friendships to this day were found outside my church context, but one of the most crucial friendships came outside my church with someone who wasn't even a pastor. As I continued to pastor a local church and lead a growing ministry to other pastors,[*] I found myself always surrounded with those who wanted me to be their pastor. I had church members looking to me as their pastor. And I had other pastors looking to me as a kind of pastor to them. I reached a point of exhaustion when I realized I needed a meaningful relationship with someone who didn't want me to pastor them.

My wife had felt the same need and had developed a meaningful friendship with another woman in our city, not a pastor's wife, who went to church across town. Her husband was a Chick-fil-A owner/operator and was a faithful church member. Having been at some group gatherings with him as a result of our wives' friendship, I reached out to see if he might want to spend some time together.

Over time, we developed a very meaningful friendship. He didn't want to talk about ministry. He didn't want to talk much about church stuff or theology. He wanted to eat hot wings, watch some football, talk a little politics, and share about our families. We talked about hobbies, other interests, and our own walks with the Lord as men. God used this friendship to show me two things about myself. First, how refreshing this friendship was to all my other relationships. Second, how much I needed a friendship like this to provide an environment of rest from all the other ministry and

---

[*] Practical Shepherding is my ministry to other pastors which I continue to lead as my primary ministry focus. For more information, go to www.practicalshepherding.com

relationships tied to it that had consumed my life. His friendship is still one of the most important in my life.

5. Calibrate expectations

Unstated and unrealistic ones can destroy a relationship, but we needn't eliminate expectations altogether. Instead, determine the relational sphere in which a friend operates and calibrate them accordingly.

James: Like everyone else, I have many different types of friends. Some operate mostly in one sphere of life while others share in the wider experience of overlap with family, church, and recreation. With some, the intimacy and vulnerability run deep but with others, things remain much closer to the surface. These distinctions don't determine the quality of the friend, but they must affect the way we evaluate it. Nearly all will know the emotional struggle that accompanies the sting of disappointment when a friend is absent or unresponsive in time of need.

We mustn't seek to escape the pain of unmet expectations by avoiding them in isolation; rather, we must learn to set them appropriately. Some people adjust them intuitively as they move in and out of relationships, but for those who struggle with feeling let-down more regularly, this area is likely a key to healthier friendships. In these circumstances, we give too little thought to relational terms but apply them unilaterally to every friend. However, learning to establish them for each person by giving careful consideration to the level of overlap and the person's margin based on stage of life and other commitments, and the amount of investment we are making in the relationship will provide a path toward longer-term friendships.

6. Seek deep connection to foster trust in one another

Unintentional, relational misfires sabotages friendships. Most often, insensitivity contributes to these problems because one or both people fail to appreciate the other person's point of view. Well before the potential for conflict arises, connect with one another to grow in understanding and compassion with each other to subvert problems before and after they occur. That deep connection cultivates a trust that enables us to say hard things to someone else.

Michael: When I was in my twenties, my closest friend, apart from my wife, was a young man named Peter. We had a midweek Bible Study that met on Tuesday evenings and over a number of years we saw great fruitfulness from it. Both of us had strong links at the time to the charismatic movement. One week, Peter told me that the following Tuesday he would be teaching on the gift of speaking in tongues and that it was the doorway to the reception of all of the other gifts. Although I did not believe this, I agreed to Peter teaching this as I was afraid to disrupt our friendship. But, after he had taught this, I felt led to tell him I disagreed with him. His response was quick and acerbic. He disagreed with me in no uncertain terms. I unwisely told him that he was acting like the leader of a cult. At that, he told me that he was done with the Bible Study and I could lead it henceforth alone. He not only ceased to be involved in the Bible Study but he also stopped attending church and categorically brought our friendship to an abrupt end. I have never been able to fully understand his reaction, but I was determined not to allow this failure of one friendship to sour me on others. I knew that friendship was essential for the good of my soul.

7. Be gracious in offense

'Good sense makes one slow to anger, and it is his glory to overlook an offense." Good friends are quick to give the benefit of the doubt, overlook minor and accidental offenses, confront humbly and lovingly, and forgive quickly and fully. Not every spark should

To read more, find *Pastoral Friendship* and other Practical Shepherding resources at

christianfocus.com

More resources from
Christian Focus and Practical Shepherding

Biblical Church Revitalization: Solutions for Dying and Divided Churches
by Brian Croft

A call to an intentional commitment to church revitalization in the face of dying and divided churches.

Collateral Damage: My Journey to Healing from My Pastor and Father's Failure
by James B. Carroll

After becoming the collateral damage from his fathers ministry, Carroll presents a highly practical book, showing the gospel as the power of God to heal, to restore, and to save.

Mea Culpa: Learning from Mistakes in the Ministry
by Kyle McClellan

Essential lessons from a wise, broken man who has lived through his mistakes and – by the grace of God – learned from them

Facing Snarls & Scowls: Preaching through Hostility, Apathy and Adversity in Church Revitalization
by Brian Croft, and James B. Carroll

Brian Croft and James Carroll share their personal stories and seek to encourage you to faithfully persevere in this Spirit–empowered, God–honoring, Christ–exalting work.

Practical
Shepherding

Helping pastors thrive in the trenches of pastoral ministry

through...

COMPREHENSIVE CARE
The Shepherd's House
Counseling Services
Pastoral Mentorship

REGIONAL COHORTS
Replant Cohorts
Women's Cohorts
Church in Hard Places Cohorts

GLOBAL CONTENT
Trench Talk Podcast
Books and Video resources
Workshops and Conferences

find out more at
practicalshepherding.com

Practical Shepherding
P.O. Box 21806
Louisville, KY 40221

Christian Focus Publications

Our mission statement –

STAYING FAITHFUL

In dependence upon God we seek to impact the world through literature faithful to His infallible Word, the Bible. Our aim is to ensure that the Lord Jesus Christ is presented as the only hope to obtain forgiveness of sin, live a useful life and look forward to heaven with Him.

Our Books are published in four imprints:

CHRISTIAN
FOCUS

popular works including biographies, commentaries, basic doctrine and Christian living.

CHRISTIAN
HERITAGE

books representing some of the best material from the rich heritage of the church.

MENTOR

books written at a level suitable for Bible College and seminary students, pastors, and other serious readers. The imprint includes commentaries, doctrinal studies, examination of current issues and church history.

CF4•K

children's books for quality Bible teaching and for all age groups: Sunday school curriculum, puzzle and activity books; personal and family devotional titles, biographies and inspirational stories – because you are never too young to know Jesus!

Christian Focus Publications Ltd,
Geanies House, Fearn, Ross-shire,
IV20 1TW, Scotland, United Kingdom.
www.christianfocus.com